Joseph Llewelyn Thomas

Journeys Among the Gentle Japs in the Summer of 1895

With a Special Chapter on the Religions of Japan

Joseph Llewelyn Thomas

Journeys Among the Gentle Japs in the Summer of 1895
With a Special Chapter on the Religions of Japan

ISBN/EAN: 9783744756099

Printed in Europe, USA, Canada, Australia, Japan

Cover: Foto ©Andreas Hilbeck / pixelio.de

More available books at **www.hansebooks.com**

JOURNEYS AMONG THE GENTLE JAPS

IN THE SUMMER OF 1895

WITH A SPECIAL CHAPTER ON THE RELIGIONS OF JAPAN

BY THE

REV. J. LL. THOMAS, M.A., F.R.G.S.
VICAR OF ABERPERGWM;
AUTHOR OF "AN UNDERGRADUATE'S TRIP TO ITALY AND ATTICA,"
"OXFORD TO PALESTINE," ETC.

WITH MAP AND A PHOTOGRAVURE PORTRAIT

LONDON
SAMPSON LOW, MARSTON & COMPANY
LIMITED
St. Dunstan's House
FETTER LANE, FLEET STREET, E.C.
1897

LONDON:
PRINTED BY WILLIAM CLOWES AND SONS, Limited,
STAMFORD STREET AND CHARING CROSS.

Dedicated

TO

MR. H. M. STANLEY, M.P., D.C.L., ETC.,

AS A HUMBLE TRIBUTE
TO HIS UNRIVALLED SERVICES
TO THE CAUSE OF GEOGRAPHICAL SCIENCE,
AND IN GRATEFUL ACKNOWLEDGMENT
OF A PERSONAL FRIENDSHIP
MUCH APPRECIATED
BY THE AUTHOR.

"This iland of Iapon is a great land, and lyeth to the northwards, in the lattitude of eight and fortie degrees, and it lyeth east by north, and west by south or west south west, two hundred and twentie English leagues. The people of this iland of Iapon are good of nature, curteous aboue measure, and valiant in warre: their justice is seuerely executed without any partialitie upon transgressors of the law. They are gouerned in great ciuilitie. I meane, not a land better gouerned in the world by ciuil policie. The people be verie superstitious in their religion, and are of diuers opinions."—*Will Adams (Seventeenth Century).*

PREFACE

When Japan emerged from her isolation forty years ago, it is not surprising that so remarkable an event should have called forth a multiplicity of books describing from every possible standpoint the country which had remained so long a sealed empire; but it would have been strange indeed if much that was written of a land with a civilisation so unique, thus thrown open to the rest of the world at one stroke of the ruler's pen, did not misrepresent the stern reality. For even now, four decades after we forced our acquaintance upon her at the cannon's mouth, Japan—as no other country in the world—is apt to run away with the sober sense of the one who sets himself to write about her. It is my wish, in preparing this volume, to guard myself against the suspicion of the same want of self-restraint and the temptation to "enthuse," and, on the other hand, not to be too niggardly in my praise of a country which—all are agreed—has a great deal about it that appeals with an irresistible charm to the Western mind. A book of first impressions of Japan must necessarily be more highly coloured than one of later and more matured opinions. For even Japan after a while begins to pall, and in revising at a later date the impressions jotted down in the first enthusiasm of landing on those strange shores, one finds it necessary to tone down here and there. But the same sort of account will not be expected from a tourist as from a returned missionary or merchant who has resided in the country for years, and has become more or less "Japanesy." This is the book of a tourist, and any old residents of the country who may read it will probably smile at much that it contains, and wonder that the writer should have been so easily charmed by what is to them unromantic and commonplace. The impressions it contains are such as they were first written down, and the narrative of the journey is but slightly altered from the form in which it was first entered in my journal.

J. LL. T.

GLYN-NEATH,
    December 21st, 1896.

CONTENTS

CHAPTER I.
	PAGE
ACROSS CANADA	1

CHAPTER II.
| THE NORTH PACIFIC. . . . . . . | 13 |

CHAPTER III.
| YOKOHAMA . . . . | 29 |

CHAPTER IV.
| KAMAKURA AND ENOSHIMA . . . . | 42 |

CHAPTER V.
| THE HAKONE HILLS . . . . . . | 58 |

CHAPTER VI.
| TÒKYÒ . . . . | 78 |

CHAPTER VII.
| TÒKYÒ (*continued*) . . . . . . | 91 |

CHAPTER VIII.
| TÒKYÒ (*continued*) . . . . . . | 103 |

CHAPTER IX.
Nikkô and Neighbourhood 116

CHAPTER X.
The Tôkaidô Line 136

CHAPTER XI.
Kobe and Neighbourhood 155

CHAPTER XII.
The Sanyô Line 172

CHAPTER XIII.
Shikoku 190

CHAPTER XIV.
Shikoku (*continued*) 204

CHAPTER XV.
The Return 221

CHAPTER XVI.
The Religions of Japan 232

Index 252

JOURNEYS AMONG THE GENTLE JAPS

CHAPTER I.

ACROSS CANADA.

Setting out—Montreal—The "C. P. R."—Rate of speed—Fellow-passengers—Mr. Yung Wing—His opinion of Li Hung Chang—General Grant and Li—The through journey—Winnipeg—North-West Mounted Police—Missionaries—Cree Indians—Moose Jaw—Medicine Hat—Calgary—The Rockies—Kicking-horse Pass—The "Great Divide"—Fearful descent—The Selkirks—Snowsheds—British Columbia—"A Thing of Beauty"—Arrival at Vancouver—A useful *vade-mecum*—The story of Vancouver—A mushroom town—From log cabins to granite palaces—Life in Vancouver—The "C. P. R." Hotel—A "dip" in the Pacific.

I HAD been travelling in the States on a journalistic commission entrusted to me by the *Western Mail*, when I found myself, somewhat unexpectedly, in a position to gratify the wish of a lifetime, and to set out for the land of the Rising Sun. Japan was then on everybody's lips. She had astonished the civilised world by the series of brilliant exploits on sea and land by which she had humiliated her hated rival in the Far East. The Americans, especially—who do not forget that it was their gunboats that forced Japan to become amenable to Western influences and to enter the comity of nations—saw in the triumph of that country the direct result of their own high-handed proceeding. Japan had suddenly proved herself a power that even the West would have to reckon with, and had gone far to establish her claim to the coveted title of "Britain of the Pacific."

On May 26th, 1895, I found myself—for the third time—at Montreal, going the round of the same sights which had charmed me so much before—again admiring the unrivalled prospect from the summit of Mount Royal, and interested as keenly as ever, as I walked through the streets and lanes of the city, in the spectacle of two races so diverse in many ways living so amicably together. The morning of the 28th I took the "cars" for Vancouver, and resigned myself to a five days and a half's unbroken experience of the famous Canadian Pacific Railway. The "C. P. R." is a great name in America. It is far and away the greatest enterprise ever undertaken and successfully carried out on that continent of big enterprises. Brooklyn Bridge and the harnessing of Niagara are mere trifles compared with it.

The Canadians are justly proud of it. It is even a great political force—being aptly nick-named "the Government on wheels." There is no more common topic on board Atlantic liners than the merits of the "C. P. R." No sooner are you out of Liverpool or Southampton than those initials strike your ear, either in the saloon, on deck, or in the smoking-room. It is not claimed for the "C. P. R." that it has annihilated distance, but it has taken a long stride forward in that direction, and will yet do more. It is impossible to forecast the ultimate development of that great system. As regards speed, the time occupied at present in the transit from terminus to terminus is five days and a few hours. Once at least the journey was done in four days, but the strain on the track was too great to justify a repetition of the experiment. It is safe to predict that before many years four days will become the normal time, and then the extreme limit of speed will perhaps have been attained, as seems to be already the case on the Atlantic. But it is not safe to lay down limits to the developments of the "C. P. R."

Several of those who boarded the train with me at Montreal journeyed with me the whole distance. In addition to English and Scandinavian land-hunters bound for the north-west, pig-tailed Chinamen and keen-eyed Japs crowded Montreal platform, and fraternised along the route, looking not at all the traditional enemies they are commonly regarded. The Japs were mostly Pullman passengers, and were either prosperous New York merchants proceeding to their country for wares, or students returning home after a course of American or European training. They presented a striking contrast to the Chinese, who were of the working class, having probably made their "pile" in the laundry line. A noticeable exception was a very respectable Chinaman, with whom I came frequently in contact during the voyage across the Pacific—a Mr. Yung Wing—who was probably the only celestial on board the train and afterwards the boat that did not sport a pig-tail. He had become completely Americanised by a long residence in the States, and had married an American wife. Indeed, but for his unmistakably Mongolian features, he might have passed for an American—or rather, I ought to say Englishman—as he betrayed no trace of an American accent, though he resided in New England (Hartford), where the Yankee characteristics are supposed to be most pronounced. He was well acquainted with Li Hung Chang, and held the opinion of him which one constantly hears expressed in the Far East—that he has been a curse rather than a blessing to China, and that he has been the one great obstacle to the development of China on Western lines. Perhaps that was charging Li with more than his due share of responsibility for the rigid conservatism of the Celestial Empire, but the famous Viceroy has no friends among those Chinese who have come under the influence of Western ideas. The one dominant principle of his career, they will tell you, has been to enrich himself and his family at the expense of the country, and he is said to have succeeded amazingly. He and his relatives between them own the greater part of a rich province. Mr. Yung Wing had nothing but ridicule for the estimate of Li formed by General Grant, who said that of the three great men whom he had met in his tour round the world, Disraeli, Bismarck, and Li Hung Chang, he was not sure that the last was not the greatest.

A journey across the American Continent without a break is not to be recommended, even with the splendid arrangements of the Canadian Pacific. It must be remembered that it is like going from London to Liverpool fourteen times, or from London to Edinburgh eight times, in one journey. A break either at Winnipeg or Banff, if not at both, is a necessity, if the journey is to be enjoyed. The pleasures of the ride through the transcendent scenery of the Rockies and the Selkirks, down the cañon of the Fraser, and, finally, along the charming woodland region of British Columbia, cannot be appreciated by the jaded senses of the through passenger. A "stop-over" at Banff will refresh the mind of the West-bound traveller for the due appreciation of the rapidly-moving pictures which will await him. I am here preaching what I did not practise, as I left Montreal too late to allow myself the benefit of a "stop-over" anywhere *en route*. The train I travelled by was the last, except one, that would take me to my destination in time for the boat for Japan, and I required a few hours at Vancouver before embarking. My advice to those of my readers who may contemplate the trip is not to follow my example, if they can help it, but to do the overland journey more at their leisure. They will have heard all about Winnipeg—that city of mushroom growth in the heart of the continent, the Hudson's Bay fort of yesterday, now a thriving city of many thousand inhabitants, the commercial focus of the north-west —and they will do well to break their journey there. No city is so often cited in illustration of the go-aheadness of life in the New World as Winnipeg. The hour's look round allowed the through passenger gives him but a vague and confused idea of that remarkable city, with its miles of imposing structures that would do credit to a city of a century's growth. From Winnipeg to the Rockies is a distance of nearly a thousand miles. Before the railway was built, this was a six weeks' journey, post haste, the old ox-trains taking something like three months. Now it is a matter of hours, not of days or weeks. Portage-la-Prairie, Brandon, Regina, Calgary, etc., are, like Winnipeg, cities of phenomenal growth, and centres of prosperous farming regions. During this section of the journey we make the acquaintance of the North-West Mounted Police, a body of men of whom Canada has reason to be proud. One or two of these red-coated guardians of the prairies are sure to join you on the "cars," and perhaps enter into a conversation with you. You will also probably encounter a missionary or two on the train. Each has a number of settlements separated by long distances to minister to, and the "C. P. R.," with characteristic consideration, allows them to travel between their mission stations for a nominal charge, or no charge at all. Specimens of Cree Indians, with their squaws and papooses, painted and blanketed, and looking very picturesque in spite of the dirt, resort to the different stations to see the trains pass through, and to trade in curios. Some of the places we come upon in the midst of the great prairies, notwithstanding their weird names, are veritable oases, and quite refresh us by their charming appearance. Moose Jaw, cut off from the rest of the world, is just such a place. Its strange appellation is an abridgment of an Indian name, meaning, "The-creek-where-the-white-man-mended-the-cart-with-a-moose-jaw-bone"—which would be even more awkward in every-day use than some of the Welsh place-names are to the average Englishman, who styles them "crack-jaw." But Moose Jaw is a remarkably smart, cheerful-looking town, with none of the uncouthness which the name would suggest. Medicine Hat is another. It is a finely situated and rapidly-growing town on the banks of the South Saskatchewan, and presents a refreshing contrast to its desert-like setting of prairie *steppes*. At Medicine Hat the train stops half-an-hour. During the interval I went with the Rector, who had travelled with me for some hours, to see his church and rectory. They were both small wooden structures, but the internal arrangements of the former were such as the most fastidious churchman would think "correct," if not particularly ornate. On the fourth morning we awoke to find ourselves entering the Rockies, Calgary—another township with a future—having been passed in the night. For three hours the long heavily-laden train kept climbing that great backbone of the American continent till it reached the summit in the Kicking-Horse Pass, a mile above the sea—the "summit," it need hardly be said, in an engineering sense, for the mountains still towered several thousand feet above us. We had no sooner passed the "Great Divide"— where two small streams, starting from a common source, part company, and flow, one into the Pacific and the other into the Atlantic—than we begin to feel that we have begun our way down the Western slope of the range. Then we realise that we are descending a fearfully steep grade, and we experience a feeling of uneasiness as to whether the heavy train is well under control. But of that there is no cause whatever for fear. Through wild and terrible scenes —which I shall not attempt to describe—over flimsy-looking trestle bridges, and through miles of snow-sheds, we are hurried along to the foot of the Rockies, and then over the parallel range, the Selkirks, till we reach the level region of British Columbia, surfeited with the sight of Nature in her most impressive aspects. Of giant hoary-headed mountains, frowning rocks, Nature's domes and spires, abysmal gorges, foaming torrents and roaring cataracts, of gleaming glaciers and snow-fields, we had had enough. We experience a feeling of relief when our train rolls into the station of Vancouver, and we catch our first glimpse of the stately steamer—with every feature of which we are already familiar, though we now see her for the first time in the flesh—which is to be our home for thirteen days on the broad Pacific. There she lay, moored in her imposing majesty at the wharf near the depôt—" a thing of beauty " and " a joy for ever," conscious, as it were, of being the pride of the people of Vancouver.

I have not mentioned what was a constant companion of my trans-continental journey, and that was an annotated time-table, which is given to every passenger on his setting out. It is a piece of railway literature which is not to be found out of the New World, and which (in that form), as far as I am aware, is only issued in connection with the " C. P. R.," but I see no reason why something like it should not be adopted in this country by our leading lines. It not only gives a brief descriptive account of all the various places and interesting sights passed, but the distance each station is from the starting-point, and the hour the train is due at each station, arranged in such a way that by looking down the time column the passenger can tell with exactness his whereabouts when he awakes out of sleep, as the train is almost invariably "on time." The publication also contains memoranda pages, on which the tourist can jot down his notes, and thus it becomes a record of his journey across.

Vancouver owes its existence entirely to the "C. P. R.," of which it is the terminus. Until May, 1886, its site was covered by the forest primeval. In a few weeks, not only had a large clearing been made among the mammoth trees, but something like a town had sprung into existence; but in July a fire, originating in the surrounding forest, swept away every house but one in the place, and, with that exception, every building now in Vancouver has been erected since that date. Handsome structures of brick and granite have taken the place of the timber houses of the first settlement. The remains of the forest are now a public park, which is one of the attractions of Vancouver. The population of the town in 1894 was twenty thousand. It has many miles of well-made streets, and, like all towns of that size on the American continent, is lighted by electricity and has electric cars. In its streets frontier and backwoods life is seen intermingled with the European, the American, and the Oriental. Down at the water's edge are extensive wharves, lined with vessels from China, Japan, Australia, and the South Sea Islands, as well as from the various American ports on the Pacific coast.

One of the finest buildings in Vancouver is the "C. P. R." Hotel, which is situated on high ground, and from which is obtained a lovely view of the town and the surrounding country.

A dip in the English Bay—which has bathing facilities equal to those of any watering-place in England—is one of my pleasant recollections of Vancouver. It was an "event," as it was my first introduction into the Pacific.

CHAPTER II.

THE NORTH PACIFIC.

Leaving Vancouver—The *Empress* steamers—Description—The *Empress of India*—A floating caravanserai—Chinese waiters—*Menu* card—English impatience—The Pacific justifies its name—Max O'Rell and the North Atlantic—Typhoons—"Westward to the Far East"—The *Empress of India* in a typhoon—The *Beaver*—The Straits of Georgia—Mount Baker—Off Victoria—The ocean voyage—Crossing the meridian—"Throwing a day overboard"—The reason why—The Aleutian Islands—Games—The Japan stream—Three "celestials" die—"Fishbones"—A lucid explanation—Ship-life of the "heathen Chinee"—Sundays on board—Impressive services—Parade—An exciting episode—Library—Japanese history—Kinka-San—Gulf of Tôkyô—Its charms—Arrival at Yokohama.

On the second day after my arrival at Vancouver I had to start on my long voyage—the longest, perhaps, without a stoppage or sight of land made by passenger steamers in any quarter of the globe. I don't know if the time will ever come when we shall hear of the "Pacific Ferry" as we do now of the "Atlantic Ferry." Certainly, the Canadian

Pacific, by their line of *Empresses*, has gone far to make such a description to some extent applicable. It is still ordinarily a voyage of twelve or thirteen days, and even the Yankee has not gone so far as to dub the Pacific a "pool." But, given a fair sea (and the Pacific is not, as is well known, so often "with its back up" as the North Atlantic) the days spent in crossing that vast wilderness of waters in one of the *Empress* boats pass away very pleasantly, and if the sight of a sail never cheers the vision, and even that of land is not always to be depended upon, and if we are cut off for a fortnight from the living world, there is never a lack of resources on board, below and above deck, to beguile the tedium of the long voyage. The three steamships composing the line— the *Empress of India*, *Empress of Japan*, and *Empress of China*—are, as they have been described, veritable floating palaces, triumphs of the art of ship-building. They certainly represent the high-water mark in marine architecture.

Though they have been frequently described, a few particulars may be given here. They are 485 feet in length and 51 feet beam; they have accommodation for 150 saloon passengers. They have a hurricane deck, cabins and state-rooms amidships, porcelain baths, watertight compartments, twin screws, triple expansion engines, capable of a speed of over nineteen knots an hour. The dining saloon and library are of the most ornate kind, the former, with its central glass dome, illuminated windows, and *vis-à-vis* family tables, suggesting a high-class American *café*. The three are of the cruiser type—to be converted into fighting ships in case of need—and are commanded by men of the Naval Reserve, most of whom are navigators of great experience.

The *Empress of India*, setting out from Vancouver June 3rd, 1895, was a floating *caravanserai* of seven hundred souls. The servants (or "boys," as they are commonly called), were chiefly Chinese, as were also a large proportion of the crew. The first sight of a number of yellow pig-tailed servitors, in caps and snowy blouses, standing in a mute row ready to enter on their duties as the passengers come in to dinner, is one that will be long remembered, and it is a view of "Celestials" under the best conditions. It is not often that they are seen so clean and presentable. Voyagers never fail to be struck with their silent automatic movements and soft velvety tread. Generally, their knowledge of English is limited to a few words of the "pidgin" dialect, and it is found necessary to number the different items on the *menu* card, so that in ordering you have only to point to the number of the dish. The name, as a rule, is beyond their comprehension, and when the name is given without the number amusing mistakes sometimes occur, the consequences of which a quick-tempered passenger or officer is apt to visit upon the head of the meek and inoffensive waiter. The Englishman or American abroad too often forgets to make allowance for the difficulties to foreigners of his own speech, which are to no race more insurmountable than to the Mongol, and—a monoglot himself—is apt to be impatient at the linguistic ignorance of other nations. That English will one day be the universal speech may be granted, but the world is not yet come to that. Meanwhile, many of our countrymen abroad will act as if it had, and rail at the stupidity of the Asiatic and the African, no less than the European, who does not speak their language.

My first passage across the Pacific was of the pleasantest, and the second was like unto it. Indeed, I don't know whether it would be possible to find the North Atlantic for thirteen days so much like the proverbial mill-pond, and then a few weeks later to find it again in the like placid mood for a similar period. For, no doubt, Max O'Rell was not far wrong when he described the North Atlantic as generally "having its back up"; and, though the North Pacific can at times belie its name and even rival the Atlantic at its worst, its normal condition is without doubt more tranquil, and Magellan had good cause for giving it the appellation he did. The typhoon season seems to be indicated by a rhyming verse which is well known in the Far East. It is as follows:—

> "June, too soon.
> July, stand by.
> August, you must.
> September, remember.
> October, all over.

Though one hears variations of it, and sometimes its correct version is a subject of animated disputes among the passengers, the above form is given on the authority of Miss Scidmore, whose little book, 'Westward to the Far East,' besides being one of the most readable little handbooks for the journey, is also one of the most reliable.

The breeding-place of the typhoon is generally in the vicinity of the Philippine Islands, whence it whirls up the Gulf of Tonquin, and then passes into the Yellow Sea and strikes the coasts of Japan. But even a typhoon is not to be seriously dreaded

C

when you are on board an *Empress* and in the open ocean. The chances are against your being at its centre. In nineteen cases out of twenty you will be on an outer circle, and even when you are exposed to the full brunt of it, a staunch boat such as those of the "C. P. R.," navigated by such experienced men as there are in that service, can weather the worst. I was shown in an officer's cabin, on board the *Empress of India*, a sketch of that boat taken when at the centre of a typhoon in the Chinese seas by a well-known artist among the passengers. It was the most terrific storm that the steamer had up to that time encountered, and if the picture was the faithful representation of the scene that the officer assured me it was, it certainly seemed incredible that even the *Empress* could have lived in such a sea. But she rode through it triumphantly, and, when beyond the circle of the typhoon, seemed as trim and taut as when she entered it. I mention this for the reassurance of timid passengers, who, as they approach Japan, will hear a great deal about the dreaded typhoon. Indeed, there are not many passages so free from dangers as that from Vancouver to Yokohama. No sail is sighted between the two shores, no iceberg floats in the North Pacific, and though some may miss the excitement of such scenes, there is the compensating advantage that your mind can be at ease as regards any chance of a collision, and you can feel in the thickest fog that you have the whole vast desert of waters practically to yourself.

There was some disappointment among the voyagers, as we were steaming out of the inlet of Vancouver and threading the Narrows, at missing a sight of the *Beaver*, or rather of her bones. The *Beaver* was the first steamer that churned Pacific waters, having been brought round the Horn in 1836 for the service of the Hudson Bay Company, and, after being incapacitated, was used as a tugboat when, in 1889, it became a wreck off Vancouver. But the remains had lately disappeared, and so the interesting sight of the earliest and latest steamships in the Pacific in juxtaposition is no longer possible.

From Vancouver to Victoria, a distance of eighty-two miles, is a land-locked passage of great beauty. The course is down the Straits of Georgia. The noble peak of Mount Baker, nearly fourteen thousand feet in height, and covered with perpetual snow, impresses us in the distance. It is night before we are off Victoria, and so we are denied even a distant glimpse of the old provincial capital which so excites the admiration of all who visit it, and which, notwithstanding the keen rivalry of Vancouver City, still boasts the title of the Queen City of the West. A few came on board at Victoria, and as soon as their belongings had been stowed away, our mammoth home moved away once more—away from the New World towards the Old, from the Far West towards the Far East, "where the sun sets, the sun rises, and time begins."

Our voyage commences at the 49th parallel of north latitude, and ends at 35° and 20' north. By keeping north, the distance is considerably lessened, and, impossible as it may seem on the map, the shortest way across would be through the Aleutian Islands, and when they have been thoroughly surveyed, that, no doubt, will be the course taken. At present, East-bound steamers get within a few miles of the southernmost of those islands, but never go north of them, though the *Parthia* once passed close to the shores of the island of Attu, well into the Behring Sea, and heard "the wolf's long howl." Why we should be taking what appeared on the map such a circuitous route puzzled some of the lady passengers not a little. It was only on the production of a globe that the pestered officers succeeded in convincing them that they were not being purposely taken out of their way. They admitted at once that it was perfectly clear. Not so clear, however, could the scientific fact be made to their unscientific minds by the most clear-headed demonstrator, that it was necessary on the voyage out to drop a day from the calendar, and on the return journey to double a day. One of the first questions asked by a sceptical lady on arriving at Yokohama, was what day it was there. It is doubtful if, after all the efforts of the officers who were plied with inquiries, any fair seeker after knowledge thoroughly grasped the fact. Not that they proved themselves more dense than the gentlemen, but the latter, as a rule, did not bother their heads about the explanation, but accepted the fact and thought no more about it. This is how one fair writer accounts for it, but whether her explanation requires to be explained, my readers must judge :—

"We left Vancouver on a Monday and reached Japan on a Monday. But the Monday between we missed out altogether. There is a puzzle for you! How could that be? If you look at a map of the world, you will see about halfway between Japan and America the 180° of longitude. That is where 'East of Greenwich' and 'West of Greenwich' join. In coming across the Atlantic and America and half of the Pacific we had each day caught up the sun a little bit, till at the 180° we were twelve hours behind English time. But coming westward to England from the East we began there at twelve hours before Greenwich time. Those twenty-four hours had to be added on to days when we were travelling westward, and we had to use up a whole day of hours, and so to make our time come right we had to drop out a day when we reached the 180°, where the sun, as it were, sets in the west and yet rises in the east. I am afraid I cannot explain it any better." *

The above is a laudable attempt, and is a distinct advance in lucidity upon the "explanation" one hears sometimes from lady voyagers, as the result of much patient instruction on the part of one of the ship's officers.

With the exception of crossing the meridian, there are not many "events" to be recorded in the passage across the North Pacific. It was our good fortune to pass comparatively close to two or three of the Aleutian Islands, but voyagers are not always sure of even a distant glimpse of land. The sight of an archipelago of which the outside world knows so little awakened keen interest among the passengers. But the islands in themselves were very uninteresting, being bleak, barren rocks, apparently uninhabited. We approached within three miles of one and took soundings. The games on board were of the usual sort, such as cricket, football, shovel-board, quoits, athletic sports, cards, dominoes, as

* 'Ever Westward through Heathen Lands,' by Edith M. E. Baring-Gould.

well as the various games of later invention. In fact, there are very few games played on land that cannot be played with greater or less inconvenience on sea. Golf has not yet, as far as I am aware, been adapted to the restricted conditions of an ocean voyage, but an enthusiastic golfer may yet be able to indulge his passion on board ship. The idea among the passengers in regulating their lives on board is to make themselves forget, as far as possible, that they are on sea and surrounded by a waste of waters. "Amusements committees" are dominated by that one idea. There were frequent dances on board. The last two were held in the open air, on the promenade deck, when we were well in the Japan Stream (for Japan has its "Gulf Stream") and the nights were warm. Just as the big dance—the farewell ball—was coming on, a poor Chinaman died. But as he was "only a Chinee," the only notice taken of the mournful event was the postponement of the ball half-an-hour to enable the doctor—one of the chief organisers— to be present at the opening. Three celestials died during the voyage, and, in accordance with the contract, their remains were embalmed and carried on to China. I may add that the bones of Chinese who have died in America often form part of the

West-bound cargo. They are generally shipped under the entry of fishbones. A pig-tailed waiter thus explained to Sir Edwin Arnold why his countrymen wished to have their remains transferred to China. "That number one pieccy God-pidgin!" said the yellow-skinned celestial; "suppose wantchee go topside, after kill, then wantchee family make chin-chin joss at grave. Suppose no takee bones, no makee grave, no speakee chin-chin joss, then not belong topside at all after kill, belong hellee." That is, the Chinese attach great importance to certain religious offices being performed in presence of the dead man's relics, or at the spot where they are buried, by surviving relatives and descendants.

There is a certain interest in studying the ship life of the "Heathen Chinee," although, when you come in contact with him in such close quarters, you are able to sympathise with the sentiment of Bret Harte:—

> "Which I wish to remark—
> And my language is plain—
> That for ways that are dark,
> And tricks that are vain,
> The heathen Chinee is peculiar."

As for the way in which our Sundays were observed, it need hardly be said that, in this respect too, every facility was given for spending our Sundays as far as possible as on land. It has been my lot to be present, and even take a prominent part, in divine service upon several occasions on sea, but I never remember a service on shipboard which so impressed me as the one in the saloon of the *Empress of India* in mid-Pacific. Everything was done in order as in the best-appointed church. The commander read the service as few laymen can, officers and men as well as passengers joined in the responses, and sang the canticles and hymns with a heartiness not usual on board ship, and there was observed throughout a general reverence that might have been deemed inseparable from worship in a sacred building. To myself (who preached) there was no grievance involved in the limitation set down as to the time which I was to occupy. It is not surprising that the longwindedness of some who "occupy the pulpit" on board our ships should make such restrictions necessary. After the service there was a parade of the men on deck. The crew numbered about two hundred, a large proportion being Chinese.

One of the exciting episodes of the passage is the practice of the crew in lowering the boats and dealing with an imaginary outbreak of fire. All were in their allotted stations a few seconds after the sounding of the alarm bell. To a nervous passenger, not warned beforehand, such violent ringing of the bell followed by such mad excitement, might prove extremely awkward. Of course, the anxiety of such an one cannot last many seconds, as it is soon found that the wild rushing to and fro is all acting, but it occurred to me, as it must occur to others, that a word might with advantage be sent round beforehand to the passengers without informing those who are to be taken unawares.

That there is a splendid library on board the *Empress* boats goes without saying, and that it is well stocked with works on China and Japan is equally a matter of course. If a Japan-bound passenger goes on board with only a general idea of the country he is visiting, and with no idea at all of its stirring history, by the time he reaches Yokohama he will know (if he be a reading man) all about the sun goddess, Ama-terasu, the divine ancestress of the Mikado; of Jingô Kôgô, the first Empress; of Kôbô Daishi, the greatest of Japanese saints; of Hideyoshi, the great general of the Middle Ages; of the Shôgun Iyeyasu, the greatest of Japanese rulers; of his grandson Iemitsu, only less famous; and various other great names which he will hear every day in the course of his peregrinations through the country. He will have learnt, perhaps for the first time, that Japan was in a fair way of being Christianised in the sixteenth century, and that traces of the Jesuit mission of that day have survived to the present time. The summary ejection of the missionaries, the practical stamping out of Christianity, the all but entire closing up of the country to the outer world, its sudden re-opening forty years ago, and its marvellous renascence since, will have interested him as a fairy tale.

The island of Kinka-zan was sighted at noon on Saturday. For twenty-four hours we skirted the Japanese coast, but saw little of it, owing to a thick haze, till we had rounded Cape Su-zaki and were steaming into the Gulf of Tôkyô. All on Sunday morning was bathed in glorious sunshine, and our approach to the Land of the Rising Sun was as it should be. None of those who were visiting Fanland for the first time were doomed to disappointment. The beauties of the Gulf of Tôkyô charmed all on board. Residents of the country—European and native alike—who were returning to their homes, pointed out to us with pride the various features of interest, to the right and to the left, as we coursed up the picturesque bay. At one moment a quaint little fishing village, at another an ancient shrine or temple, at another a many-storied pagoda excites our enthusiasm. Proceeding on our way through a fleet of galley-like junks and graceful sampans, of modern war-ships and merchant steamers, we arrive at length at our moorings, and at noon are fast to the company's buoy, and are encircled by Japan. Steam launches bear down upon us, the deck is rapidly over-run with natives and European and American residents, and amid many leave-takings I take my place, along with my few *impedimenta*, in a spick-and-span sampan, and am sculled ashore by a muscular little Jap, whose only garment is a breech-clout.

CHAPTER III.

YOKOHAMA.

Landing in Japan—Custom House examination—The *Jinrickisha*—Coolies—Some scions of the nobility—Fares—The Queen's English in Japan—Old Japan at Yokohama—Hotels—The Bluff Population—Clubs—Public hall—An American "star"—Churches—Seamen's mission room—Currency—Mysterious notes—Railways—Carriages—The natives as fellow-passengers—Commissariat—Fares—Luggage—Officials—"Treaty ports"—Passport regulations—A recent change.

WE are on Japanese soil. The examination at the Custom House is a mere formality. The attempt to smuggle opium alone can cause any real trouble. Even Japanese officials, the pink of politeness and courtesy as they are, and ever with a smile of welcome for the foreigner who lands on the shores from which he was so long excluded, can scowl at the sight of the contraband drug. Landing in the Far East is not the ordeal it is in the East, notably at Jaffa. The sight of a fleet of sampans racing to meet the incoming steamer need strike no terror into the heart of the timid tourist, like that caused by the notorious boatmen of Syria. The Jap is the exact antithesis of the Arab—the maritime as well as the inland type.

A row of coolies with their *jinrickishas* is in waiting on the landing-stage—not the noisy, pestilent tribe which is ready to pounce upon the new arrival in some ports nearer home. Though each tries to be the first to arrest the attention of the new-comer, there is no unseemly wrangling, no angry disputing. The competition is friendly and good-humoured.

The national vehicle of Japan—which suggests an overgrown perambulator—is tolerably well known by this time to English readers, but it is not generally known that it did not originate with the Japanese, but was introduced among them by an American about thirty years ago. The assimilative Japs were so taken up with it that its use soon became general. It is now found throughout the different islands which compose the Empire, and the district is very outlandish indeed where there is not a *jinrickisha*. Every village where the road is at all practicable boasts a number of them. Besides those for public hire, many of the well-to-do Japanese have private *jinrickishas*. One hears a good deal of the powers of endurance of the coolie, but very exaggerated accounts are sometimes given. He is not the being of almost superhuman powers which he is sometimes represented to be. An occasional one is met with who will bound along a great distance with more than an ordinary load of humanity after him, and at the end of the journey exhibit very little fatigue, but he is rather the exception. Very many seem ill-fitted for such a laborious way of earning a living, either having seen their best days and worn themselves out in the service, or having never had a strong constitution to start with. More than once did I hesitate to employ a coolie on the ground of his generally emasculated appearance, and thought it a doubtful kindness to give him a job. But many, on the other hand, are full of vigour, and, although there is a certain uneasy feeling at first in allowing oneself to be drawn along by a human being in a shaft, an occasional one is so very muscular and able-bodied that disquieting thoughts of countenancing a form of slavery do not obtrude themselves. It is said that there are found in the ranks of the coolies scions of some of the noblest houses of Japan. How far that is true I don't know, but members of the old *samurai* or retainer class, who were disbanded at the fall of the feudal system, seem to be plentiful enough among them. Just as there are said to be two or three baronets, and others with handles to their names, among London cabbies, so among the *jin-rickisha*-men of Tôkyô, rumour says, there are members of the titled nobility of the country. That a broken-down baronet or the son of a baronet should in his distress take to running a cab is not so very surprising, if he delights in horseflesh, as by so doing, in addition to making a living, he gratifies a passion, but we can only suppose that a Japanese count or the son of a count (for Japan has, among its western innovations, our titles) takes to the profession in order to gain a livelihood. The coolie service can offer no other attraction, though sometimes a coolie of exceptional muscle seems to take a positive delight, like a well-conditioned horse, in bounding along with his human load at the top of his speed. But to men with an inferior physique the service cannot be otherwise than very killing, and the prematurely decrepit appearance of many of them is not surprising. I have written here of the *genus* at some length, as I may not revert to the subject beyond making casual references. A few particulars as to fares may be added. At *jinrickisha* stands there is a tariff hung up on a conspicuous board. Generally, even in the interior, the information is given in English as well as in the vernacular, and very amusing specimens of the

Queen's English are sometimes seen, the work of some local student too confident in his own proficiency to submit his translation for revision to an Englishman. The fare for a short distance is nominally five *sen* (cent), but double that is expected of foreigners and is recognised as the regular charge. In fact, there is practically one tariff for the native and one for the foreigner. The charge, as given on the tariff board, is ten *sen* by the hour and seventy-five *sen* by the day, but a *pourboire* of quite an equal amount is expected of foreigners. If the Japanese coolie is not quite so rapacious as the European cabby or the American hackman, he knows how to grumble when the fare offered is only the bare amount due. But it is not often, probably, that he has occasion to grumble, as there is no class of men in or out of Japan to whom one gives a gratuity with greater pleasure.

Yokohama has by this time become to a great extent Europeanised or Americanised, but there is still a good deal of old Japan left, and is likely to remain for a long time to come. It is possible to see, in the course of a stroll through the native quarter, almost every phase of Japanese life with which we have been familiarised by fan, or tray, or screen. The visitor is fascinated by a succession of living Japanese tableaux.

There are three leading hotels in Yokohama, namely, the Grand Hotel and the Club Hotel, facing the Bund, or sea-wall, and the Oriental, at the back of the Grand, in Main Street, all within a convenient distance of the landing-place. Each seems as well appointed as any hotel of their class in Europe. My experience of hotels in the Far East did not commence till I arrived at Tôkyô. I put up at a private boarding-house on the Bluff, the landlady of which (Miss Brittan) proved to be a native of my own county. The house is one of two or three in Japan which are primarily designed for the accommodation of missionaries and their families, and is thoroughly comfortable. The Bluff, on which most of the well-to-do residents have their elegant villas and bungalows, commands a beautiful view of the Bay, and there is ample compensation for the rather steep climb. Not that Europeans and Americans often *walk* up the Bluff. They must generally hail a *jinrickisha*, for which (unless the load is unusually light) a single coolie is not sufficient, the assistance of an *atoshi*, or pusher, being necessary. Some of our countrymen and countrywomen in Japan think it out of the question to go even half a mile on foot. You are almost everywhere, in the towns, within hailing distance of a *rickisha*, and, the charge being so reasonable, walking with many becomes the exception.

The foreign population of Yokohama, according to the last official census, was 3,700, but that number included 2,471 Chinese. The British residents numbered 616, the American 187, the German 170, and the French 101. In the Yokohama United Club the British and American residents have a splendid centre of social intercourse, and the library is one of the most complete in the Far East. Other clubs are the Club Germania, the Masonic Temple, and the Chess Club. Yokohama also possesses a fine public hall, where theatrical and other entertainments are given, and where an occasional star of English or American celebrity appears. It may not always pay a distinguished *artiste* to go on tour through Japan, but when the visit is one primarily of pleasure and sight-seeing a little business may be conveniently combined with it. A lady of eminence in the American musical world made her public appearance at Kobe during my stay there, but if she came out to Japan with a view to making money, it is to be feared, from the attendance at her concerts at that port, that her speculation proved a bad one.

The spiritual interests of the Western colony are by no means neglected. The Anglican Church is well represented there, as well as the Congregationalists, the Methodists, and the Roman Catholics. An excellent institution in the foreign settlement is the Seamen's Mission Room, under the charge of the Rev. W. T. Austin, the Chaplain. The reading-room is the best I have come upon in any foreign port, far or near, and must prove a boon to our seamen which they do not often find. I turned in every day during my stay in the port (for, though not a seaman, I was assured of a welcome), and always found it well patronised.

The Japanese currency, strange as the money seems at first, is soon mastered. It is on the decimal system, and consists of the *yen* as the unit (which, at par, corresponds to the American dollar), the *sen* (or cent, the hundredth part of a *yen*), and the *rin* (the tenth of a *sen*). There are paper notes of 1, 5, and 10 *yen* and upward, as well as of 20 *sen* and 50 *sen*. Gold is practically never seen. The silver pieces are 1 *yen*, 50 *sen*, 20 *sen*, 10 *sen*, and 5 *sen*. There is also a nickel piece of 5 *sen*. The copper pieces are 2 *sen*, 1 *sen*, 5 *rin*, and 1 *rin*. The *rin* is a peculiar-looking coin, having a square hole in the centre. The value of the *yen* is based on the fluctuating value of the Mexican silver dollar, which is the monetary unit throughout the Far East. Some of the notes have their value indicated in English as well as in the language of the country, but where this is not the case, the Englishman stares at the note with as little profit as he would at Cleopatra's Needle till some kind friend enlightens him. I was congratulating myself upon the rapidity with which I thought I had mastered the currency when, on booking myself for my first railway journey in the country, I was handed as change a number of notes, all in Chinese or Japanese characters, in which I looked in vain for a single European letter or figure. There was no time to find out if the change was correct, and, besides, the booking-clerk knew no English. I had not yet had occasion to put to a practical test my stock of Japanese acquired on the journey out.

Nothing perhaps will surprise the English visitor to Japan so much as the rapid development in that country of railway locomotion. Railways now connect all the principal cities, and there were, in 1892, 1,717 miles of road, and 609 miles in course of construction. The first lines were built by English engineers, and for some years were worked by Englishmen, but all the railway systems of the country are now entirely in the hands of natives. The carriages consist of three compartments, the second class being comfortable enough for travelling short distances. As the rate of speed is much slower than it is on our own railways (the gauge is slightly narrower), a journey of two or three hundred miles would be fatiguing in the second, and the first (in which there is generally ample room) is recommended to Englishmen for a journey of that length. The Japs are inveterate railway travellers, but they make very little use of the first, and not very much of the second. Into the third they crowd like cattle, but travelling in the third with the Japs (as an Englishman will sometimes do either from motives of economy, or in order to gain a closer acquaintance with the people) is far more comfortable than travelling among the peasantry on the continent of Europe. The compartment may be more primitive and the seats harder than in Europe, but one's fellow-travellers are more innately gentle and more studious of the comfort of others than Europeans of the same class. European residents of the country may have a different tale to tell, but I must speak of the people as I found them, and I say that, during my two months' travelling, I found myself on various occasions, when making a short journey, in a third class carriage, and, though I was eyed with a great deal of curiosity, the courtesy of my fellow-passengers made the journey always a pleasant one. There are as yet no sleeping-cars or dining-cars, but neat little boxes of Japanese food are brought round at all the principal stations. A potful of tea (including, besides the pot, a tiny cup) may be had for a few *sen*. But the commissariat department on Japanese railways has yet to be developed, and the European traveller who goes a long distance is obliged, if he has not become reconciled to Japanese food, to take his own along with him.

The fares are on the general basis of three *sen* per mile for first class, two for second class, and one for third class.

Luggage is checked as in America, first-class passengers being allowed 100 pounds free, and second class passengers 60 pounds, but it need hardly be said that, among such a kind-hearted people, a slight excess is taken no account of. Officiousness is not a characteristic of Japanese officials. I must say that from my first acquaintance with Japanese railway officials, when I first entered the station at Yokohama and beheld a sight which I shall not soon forget—a platform almost covered with squatting figures, as if standing out from one vast screen, who all stood up as one man, and hurried along with clattering clogs that resounded through the whole building as soon as the train came in—till my last experience of them at the same station two months later, I found every station-master, booking-clerk, guard and porter, in fact, as well as in name, a servant of the public.

Travelling beyond the limits of the open ports (or "Treaty Ports," namely, Yokohama, Kobe, Osaka, Nagasaki, Hakodate, and Niigata) is still strictly forbidden the foreigner who is not fortified with a passport. The free limit is a radius of 10 *ri* (nearly 24½ miles) from each port. As Tôkyô is within that radius of Yokohama, it is practically, like the latter, an open port, and may be visited without a permit. It would be quite futile to try to evade the passport regulations. The system is much more real and exacting than it is in any European country or in Asiatic Turkey. When the foreigner books himself to any point beyond the free limit, he is asked for his *menjô*, and it has to be produced on his arrival at a native inn, and may be demanded by any police officer on the journey. A change occurred in the passport regulations about the time of my arrival which did away with a great inconvenience. Up to that time it was necessary to name in the document the places which the traveller intended visiting. To deviate from the route marked out beforehand was then impossible. My passport was one of the first issued under the new regulations, which made the passport one of general use for the whole country. Application for a passport has to be made through one's consul, who obtains it from the Foreign Office at Tôkyô. Three months is the maximum time for which it is usually granted, but upon its expiration it may be renewed. British subjects are charged by their Consul two dollars for a passport, while Americans only pay a few cents.

CHAPTER IV.

KAMAKURA AND ENOSHIMA.

"Midzu"—The Tôkaidô railway—Disorganised service—Scene at Yokohama station—Japanese railway stations—The favoured foreign language—"Three little maids from school"?—Will Adams and the ladies—Intense blackness of the ladies' hair—How Sir Edwin Arnold describes it—The Japanese and European complexion—A student—Interviewer and interviewed—Arrival at Kamakura—Story of an ancient capital—A Mongolian "Armada"—Kublai Khan—A Japanese "Bayeux tapestry"—Temple of Hachiman—Venerable tree—"Pure Shintô"—The Dai Butsu—A few dimensions—Seeing the wild beast feeding—A good-natured crowd—An amusing "*lapsus linguæ*"—Village chartographers—Reception of a famous American—Temple of Kwannon—*En route* to Enoshima—Katase and Koshigoe—Welcome at a *yadoya*—Entering a Japanese house—A native "interpreter"—A Japanese diet—Enoshima—Benten—A hitch—Moralising—A ride (or drive?) to Fujisawa—A romance—A faithful courtesan—Return to Yokohama.

My first excursion from Yokohama was to Kamakura and Enoshima, for which no passport was required. It was but a day's outing, for which Midzu ("cold water"), the native servant at the house, who was said to "know English," provided me with some excellent luncheon (*bentô*) wrapped up in the artistic paper of the country. My route was along the Tôkaidô Railway, which connects Tôkyô with Kyôtô. Though there were ordinarily frequent trains between Yokohama and Kamakura, the return of the troops from the seat of war had for some time so disorganised the usual arrangements that it was quite impossible to find out much in advance when a train for the general public would be available. I was told not to put my faith in time-tables, but to go to the station immediately after breakfast and there wait patiently for a train whenever the authorities would see their way to put one on. That I did, and was considered fortunate at being only kept waiting two hours and a half. But finding myself in a Japanese station for the first time, surrounded by a crowd of the happiest little people in the world, I was never at a loss for subject-matter for study, and even two hours and a half passed away quite pleasantly. At length the word went round that a train was about to proceed West, and the excitement among the good-natured, slant-eyed, picturesque company whom I had been watching with such keen interest, and the good-humoured competition for the best seats, were a sight to behold. The fare, second class, to Kamakura was 30 *sen*. The ticket was of the English card pattern, with the class and the destination in English. Some directions for passengers were in English, such as "Way Out," "Waiting Room," and the station was quite European. But in many of the stations in the interior, the only information intelligible to a European was the name of the station on the platform in Roman characters, which always appeared above or beneath the name in Japanese. One looked in vain for anything else that was legible, either on the train or in the station. Still, an Englishmen must find it much easier to travel in Japan than any other European. When any public information is given in any European language as well as in Japanese it is almost invariably in English. French and Italian are seen, but very rarely.

Sharing my compartment were three dainty Japanese maidens—"three little maids from school" they looked like. How exactly Will Adams's description of nearly three centuries ago applies to Japanese ladies now! This is how that observant old seaman found them: "Their haire very blacke and very long, tyed vp in a knot vpon the crowne in a comely manner: their heads no where shaven as the men's are. They were well faced, handed, and footed; cleare skind and white, but wanting colour, which they amend by arte; of stature low . . . very curteous in behaviour; not ignorant of the respect to be giuen vnto persons according to their fashion." Some writers have not been content with describing the hair of Japanese women as "very blacke," as quaint Will Adams does. The blackness is such that they cannot lay too much stress upon its intensity, and the resources of our language seem to fail them in conveying an adequate idea of its depth. This is how Sir Edwin Arnold describes it, and if his language does not do full justice to it, no one can hope to succeed where such a master has failed: "His palette had not any black pigments black enough to represent the night-dark depths of the tresses of the Japanese girl. Those puffed and perfumed *bandeaux* of oiled *coiffure*, so carefully dressed, and arranged so that no single hair strays from the rigid splendour of the toilette room, would make a jetty spot on the heart of midnight. So black that the very highest lights of it are blue-black beyond inky blackness; black, so that ebony would be grey beside it. The glittering tenebrosity of it makes her little visage and her little nape and throat emerge like dyed ivory from the contrast." The Japanese, on the other hand, do not experience the same difficulty in describing the complexion of Europeans. All Europeans whose hair is not positively black are one and all to the Japanese "red." They make no distinction, though their language is quite capable of it. According to Sir Edwin Arnold, they would be right in calling even a dark-complexioned Englishman "grey," compared with the "night-dark" tenebrosity of the hair of their own womenkind.

But to return to the three demure little maids who shared my compartment *en route* to Kamakura. With them were two students, one of whom was on speaking terms with my own language. Such an opportunity of airing his knowledge of English was not to be missed. He plied me with a string of questions about my country, about myself personally, about my journey out, and asked me for my impressions of Japan, on the shores of which I had only landed a few hours before. Having answered him according to the tenor of his words, I in turn became the interviewer. Education, religion, politics, were each touched upon till the train drew up at Ofuna Junction, where I had to leave the Tôkaidô and take to a branch line. Cards were exchanged (an inevitable formality under such circumstances in Japan), and the hope expressed on both sides that we should one day meet in far-away England. It is the dream of every Japanese student to be privileged some day to visit England and America, and no Englishman cherishes the fond hope of one day seeing the countries of the Far East more than many an educated Jap looks forward to a visit to those of the Far West.

A few minutes' ride along the branch line brought me to the station of Kamakura, and, ranged in a semi-circle outside the station, were a number of *jinrickishas* to convey the passengers to the historic sights—all some distance away—of Kamakura. I, however, elected to walk on this my first excursion into the country of Japan, and in twenty minutes arrived on the beach.

Kamakura, which is now, save for a few interesting relics of antiquity, an insignificant sea-side village, was once the capital of eastern Japan, and is said to have at one time contained over a million people. At Kamakura the Shogun Yoritomo, at the end of the twelfth century, laid the foundation of that military feudalism which bore so many points of resemblance to the English feudal system, and which only came to an end with the Revolution of 1868. Some of the stirring events in Japanese history occurred on the spot which I had now reached, and which presented so striking a contrast to its former troubled state. That peaceful scene was the arena of many a sanguinary feud between rival military factions. On that sea-shore were beheaded the ambassadors of Kublai Khan, whose attempt to invade Japan in the thirteenth century is remarkable as being the last made by a foreign foe. For Japanese history has its "Armada" episode, not less stirring than that of our own history. In 1259 A.D. Kublai Khan—till then invincible—invaded the coasts of Japan with an armed host of 150,000 men and a vast fleet of ships and boats; but the elements, not less than the courage of the Japanese, wrought havoc among the Mongolian "Armada," and large numbers of the men were captured and beheaded. Our distinguished countryman, Sir Edwin Arnold, who has written with such fascination of Japan, was the means of a most interesting contemporaneous illustration of that event being placed in safe custody in the Royal Archives. It was painted on a silken scroll, and was brought under Sir Edwin Arnold's notice at Tôkyô by some natives of high rank and offered to him for sale at his own price. Sir Edwin, comparing it to our own Bayeux Tapestry, told them that it ought not to be allowed to leave the country, and sent them to the palace with a letter to the Imperial secretary. It was submitted to the Mikado, who, after thoroughly inspecting it, ordered it to be deposited in the Royal

Archives, and paid a handsome sum for it to the owners.

Kamakura seems to have been repeatedly destroyed and as often rebuilt, till, early in the seventeenth century, it was completely ruined, and Yedo became the capital. The chief and almost the only remains that survive to attest its former greatness are the Temple of Hachiman, the God of War (containing several famous relics), the colossal bronze statue of Buddha—the Dai-Butsu—and the image of the so-called Thousand-Handed Kwannon, the Goddess of Mercy.

The first, dating from the end of the twelfth century, occupies a commanding position on a hill and is approached by an imposing avenue leading up from the sea. One tree, nearly twenty feet in circumference, is supposed to be twelve hundred years old. The main temple stands at the head of a flight of stone steps. Destroyed by fire early in the century, it was rebuilt in the year 1828 in the *Ryobu Shintô*, or mixed *Shintô* (*i.e.*, native) and Buddhist (*i.e.*, Indian) style, having red pillars, beams, and rafters, and adorned with painted carvings of birds and animals. I propose to describe briefly in a special chapter the religious systems of Japan, and shall there have occasion to refer to the important reform which resulted from the Revolution of 1868, by which Shintô was purged of its Buddhist accretions, and a return made to the "pure Shintô" of the early ages. The Temple of Hachiman, like many others, was despoiled of much of its beauty by the zeal of the reformers, who aimed at a severe simplicity of style.

But the chief sight of Kamakura, as, indeed, it is one of the chief sights of Japan, is the Dai-Butsu, which is the most famous of Japanese works of art. Some of the dimensions, as given by *Murray*, will give my readers some idea of its massiveness. They are as follows: height, 49 feet 7 inches; circumference, 97 feet 2 inches; length of face, 8 feet 5 inches; length of eye, 3 feet 11 inches; length of ear, 6 feet 6 inches; width of mouth, 3 feet 2 inches; circumference of thumb, 3 feet. The image is of bronze, and is supposed to have been cast in 1252. In the interior of it is a small shrine. Visitors often get photographed seated in the lap or on the thumb of the image. Professor Basil Chamberlain, the great Japanese scholar, says of it that "no other gives such an impression of majesty, or so truly symbolises the central idea of Buddhism—the intellectual calm which comes of perfected knowledge and the subjugation of all passion."

During an interval in my round of sight-seeing at Kamakura, I sat down in front of a tea-house to dispose of my *bentô* (lunch). Soon there flocked around to see the wild beast feeding a number of the villagers, young and old, but their evident good humour made their presence pleasing rather than offensive. I sincerely lamented my inability to understand and appreciate the jokes which I felt were being cracked at my expense by the wits in the crowd. Not only my person, but my actions supplied a tempting field for the exercise of their humorous faculty. When, for instance, to quench my thirst, I was handed by the bewildered waiting-maid a tumblerful of *hot* water because I had ordered "*o-yu*" (hot water) instead of "*midzu*" (cold water), the merriment of the company knew no bounds. Two squatted down with me on the bench, and were very much interested in my guide-book, especially in the map of Japan. Though the names on the map were as strange to them as the *Hiragana* characters are to an Englishman, one of them soon succeeded in putting his finger upon the position of Kamakura, and his pride (as far as a Jap can be said to have pride) in pointing out his discovery to others less intelligent than himself was natural enough under the circumstances. I had another proof later in the day of the intelligence of the natives as displayed in the use of maps and plans. A coolie, in trying to convey to me an idea of the position of a place which I wished to visit, drew on the ground a rough sketch of Kamakura and the immediate neighbourhood, and marked the site very precisely (as I afterwards found). The main roads, the coastline, the Dai-Butsu, and the Temple of Hachiman, were given with the precision of a scientific chartographer. One was inclined to echo the sentiment of the famous American who, on landing at Yokohama, and hearing himself greeted by the crowd, to his great surprise, with shouts of "*ohayo!*" (good morning), and thinking that they were honouring his native state—Ohio—exclaimed, "These little Japs are a wonderful people!"

The Temple of Kwannon stands not far from the Dai-Butsu, on a hill commanding a fine view of Kamakura and the sea. The temple is celebrated for a gold-gilt figure of Kwannon, the Goddess of Mercy, which is over thirty feet high.

From Kamakura I walked along a road skirting the shore to Enoshima—four miles distant—passing through two small villages called Katase and Koshigoe. The whole route was no less historical than picturesque. When Kamakura was at the height of its glory, this—one of the chief approaches to the city—was the scene of many events of stirring interest. At the hamlet of Katase I had to leave the road and walk across a long stretch of sand, and over an arm of the sea by a bamboo bridge, till I entered the one street which constitutes the village of Enoshima. After trying one *yadoya* (inn) recommended to me, and failing to attract attention, I made for another (*Ebisu-ya*), where I was received with such a welcome as I had read of in books on Japan, but now experienced for the first time. Who will forget his first reception at a Japanese inn—the soft melodious chorus of "*ohayos!*" the lowly prostrations on knees and noses by host, hostess and waiting-maids, the exquisite politeness of the whole *personnel* of the house, and the competition among the merry-hearted *mousmés* for the honour of unlacing the "honourable guest's" boots? Generally, the visitor has to do that operation himself, in the last resort, owing to the maids' want of acquaintance with his peculiar foot-gear. The necessity of taking off one's boots on entering a Japanese house may be irksome, but the foreigner would be a bore indeed who would think of stepping on those immaculately clean mats with his boots on. There is no need to be told the custom of the country in that respect: instinct alone would cause the traveller, not absolutely boorish, to doff his shoes. We must not forget that those beautiful mats are the chairs and tables and couches of the country. What should we say if a man came into our drawing-room and went upon our chairs and sofas with his boots on? We should probably resent it much more angrily than the kind-hearted, good-natured Jap would resent the soiling by a European boor of the soft, clean *tatamis* of his house. Still, the offence would be the same. The Japanese cannot understand the custom which they are told prevails in the Far West, of making a street or a pavement of the interior of a dwelling.

None of the natives who almost embarrassed me with their attentions at the *Ebisu-ya* knew a word of English, but a neighbour was sent for who, no doubt, was looked up to by his fellow-villagers as a wonderful linguist, but who, as an English interpreter, was absolutely worthless. He did not know as much of my language as I did of his. However, I had no serious difficulty in making my wants known. A meal was set before me, but, hungry though I was, I had not yet been long enough in the country to relish the delicacies of a purely Japanese diet. I had to be content with merely appeasing my hunger, and looking forward to a good English supper at Yokohama after my day's sight-seeing were over. Amid a general chorus of "*sayonáras*" (farewell), and the "Please come again" of the "interpreter," I took my departure, and set out to "do" Enoshima.

As I have said, Enoshima practically consists of one street, the shops of which are stocked with the sea-shells, corals, rope-sponges, and other marine curios for which the locality is celebrated. From earliest times Enoshima has been sacred to Benten, the Goddess of Luck in the Buddhist pantheon. On the far side of the island is a large cave, said to be 370 feet in depth, associated in the mythology of the country with a savage monster that used to devour the children of the village of Koshigoe, till Benten, coming down from the clouds, married him. There are several temples on the island, all more or less interesting.

Retracing my way back to Katase, I took a *kuruma* for Fujisawa, on the Tôkaidô Railway, about three miles off. At one time it looked as if I should have to do the journey on foot, and thus run the risk of missing the last train for Yokohama. The owner of the *kuruma* demanded more than double the right fare. I appealed to the tariff-board facing us, on which the precise charge was given in English and Japanese. The usual crowd of natives gathered round, but though the disputants were a countryman and a foreigner, no particular sympathy, as far as I could make out, was displayed with the former. Their crowding round was due to mere curiosity, and when the foreigner carried his point, and the native yielded under protest, their friendly attitude towards me was quite unaffected by the result, and to my "*sayonára*" they responded in unison and with evident heartiness "*sayonára*." Incidents of that kind in Japan cannot fail to set one moralising and contrasting the conduct of the Japanese with that of Europeans under similar circumstances, to the decided disadvantage of the latter.

Off the *kuruma-ya*—a mere stripling, but sturdy notwithstanding—trundled at a sharp trot, along an interesting, and, for the most part, shaded road, and in half-an-hour drew up at a tea-house, near the station of Fujisawa. A few biscuits and some lemonade—in addition to the not very relishable tea—were all that I could get, for love or money, to satisfy the inner man; but they were welcome as far as they went, and the hour before my train was spent in strolling about the village. Though Fujisawa has no particular attractions, it has its romance, for in it are shown the tombs of Oguri Hangwan, and a courtesan of the village, Terute Hime by name, of whom the following stories are told. A conspiracy to drug him with *sakè*, and then murder him, was made known by Terute Hime to Oguri Hangwan, who thereupon vaulted upon the back of a wild horse, which he had seized, and escaped to Fujisawa. On another occasion, his enemies having decoyed him into a poisonous bath which induced leprosy, his mistress —more faithful than Samson's—wheeled him in a barrow all the way to the famous sulphur springs of Yunomine, in Kishu, where a week's bathing restored him to health and strength.

Leaving Fujisawa at nine, I arrived at Yokohama a little before ten, having completed in one day an excursion to which two days are usually devoted.

CHAPTER V.

THE HAKONE HILLS.

Earthquake — Seismological Society — Earthquake drill — A popular idea — The next volcano — Passport — An official fiction — Provisions — Kodzu — Reception of a hero of the war — Squatting — One effect of railways — The Jap as a fellow-traveller — As a smoker — Tea-house — A long tram-ride — The Tôkaidô — Odawara — "Odawara Conference" — Castle — Yumoto — Tonosawa — A charming *yadoya* — *Hibachi* — O Ewa San — Embarrassing attention — O Kco San — Intruders — The *Bâyô* — Early rising — The Hon. Miss Ewa takes a seat — Rare luxury — Bathing — A week in a bath! — Cleanliness before Godliness — Evading a toll — Miyanoshita — Fuji-ya — Special industry — *Kagos* — Ashi-noyu — Matsuzaka-ya — His Japanese wife — A French journalist and Japanese ladies — Miss Bacon's testimony — Looking down upon Hakone — Return journey — Uncertainty of trains — Tôkyô.

A FAVOURITE holiday resort of the foreign residents of Yokohama and Tôkyô, is the Hakone district, to which I made an excursion two days later. As I was preparing to set out for the station, immediately after "tiffin," Yokohama was visited by an earthquake, which, although it caused comparatively little excitement among the residents, was decidedly disquieting to a new-comer. Though there is said to be on an average one earthquake a day in Japan (and probably that is an exaggeration) most of them are only registered by delicate instruments—seismometer, seismograph, or seismophone—and the inhabitants have no knowledge of them. But the tremor which agitated Yokohama that day was unpleasantly perceptible, and if it had happened in England, would have caused considerable stir. It happened on the anniversary of the day on which an unusually violent earthquake had occurred in eastern Japan the year before, by which some lives were lost, and there was a popular presentiment that another was going to happen that day. But for that general anticipation, which had wrought upon the nerves of the more timid ones, the event would have caused no excitement whatever. It is well-known that Japan is pre-eminently a land of earthquakes, being, next to the Philippine Islands, the most unstable country, physically, of any in the world. You never know at what moment you may have to rush out of the house, to get beyond the range of falling timbers, and there is the danger, when you have got clear, of disappearing in a gaping fissure in the earth. But many of the best educated

Japanese show themselves wonderfully cool in face of the danger, and seem bent more upon taking accurate notes of the phenomena with watch and instrument, and acting upon the instructions circulated by the Seismological Society, than upon looking after their personal safety. But the first impulse of the mass of the people is still to rush out of doors, and familiarity with earthquakes has only made them the more alive to the danger. It is said that the people are taught from childhood a regular earthquake drill. If the house be open when the first tremor comes, the occupants rush out of doors helter-skelter; but if it be closed, each man or woman or child takes hold of one of the *mado* (outer shutters), and rushes away with it on his or her head, as a protection from falling tiles, and as soon as the nearest open space is reached, lays it on the ground and sits on it, thereby minimising the danger of falling into cracks in the earth's surface. There is a popular idea that ground on which bamboo grows is less likely to be rent than open land, the interlacing roots being supposed to hold the ground together, and bamboo groves are consequently said to be much sought by a panic-stricken populace on the occasion of an earthquake. The deduction has been made from a large number of scientific observations of seismic phenomena that a certain spot very near Yokohama will be the site of the next volcano, which is to rise, Fuji-like, from the plain. It was fortunate that I did not know that at the time of the tremor in Yokohama, or I might have thought that the anticipation was about to be realised.

For the Hakone Hills a passport was required, which I obtained at the local Kencho (prefecture) by applying through the British Consulate. Though I never felt in better health, or looked it, than when I presented myself at the office of the Kencho with a paper from the consul, a native clerk, in handing me the passport, informed me in broken English and with a smile, that the document stated that I was visiting the Hakone District for the benefit of my health—a figment for which I was in no way responsible. If I had not acquiesced in the official fiction, the district I wished to visit would have been forbidden ground to me. At first I did not like the idea of carrying about with me a palpable lie. Anyone would have voted me a fool if I had made a difficulty about it. I did as others do, and pocketed the document, though its wording was quite belied by my appearance. Having stocked my portmanteau with a pot of Liebig's extract of meat, three tins of sardines, a small tin of biscuits, and some tea, coffee, and sugar (not omitting a knife and fork and a spoon), I set out again for the Tôkaidô Station, and, amid the deafening clatter of fellow-passengers, took my seat in a second-class compartment (fare, 62 *sen*) for Kodzu, distant forty-nine miles. As I passed again through Fujisawa, I found the platform crowded with people, among whom were the school-children drawn up in a line in charge of their teachers. As soon as the train drew up, a hearty cheer went up from the crowd, and out of one of the carriages stepped a smart young army officer, who, after exchanging greeting with some of his friends, walked off the platform escorted by the people, several of whom carried banners on long bamboo poles. There was no one in my compartment to offer me an explanation of the demonstration, but it was scarcely needed. It was the first of many similar demonstrations which I was destined to witness at railway stations in the course of my travels through the country, and the person honoured in each case was a local hero returning from the war. In every such public reception the village school-children played a conspicuous part. They were drawn up in lines, sometimes three or four deep, and, as soon as they caught sight of the hero of the hour, three hearty cheers in true British style greeted his arrival. Thus was the military spirit fostered and encouraged in the breast of young Japan.

It will probably take another generation at least before sitting down becomes quite natural to the majority of the Japanese. In railway carriages, even in the second-class, a native will often take off his shoes and squat on the seat, instead of sitting on it in Western fashion. In the third-class, among the peasantry, that is common enough. The railways, perhaps, as they spread over the country, will have more effect in making the Japanese a nation of sitters, instead of a nation of squatters and kneelers, than any other Western innovation; but it will be long before even railway travelling will quite reconcile the mass of the people to the habit of sitting. But whether sitting, squatting, or kneeling, the Jap is not to be surpassed as a companionable fellow-passenger. His innate politeness and never-failing courtesy prevent his taking more than his due share of the seat, and he will subject himself to much inconvenience and even discomfort in order to oblige others in the matter of ventilation, and if he does not ask you if you object to smoking, it is because he has never heard of anyone who *does* object. He belongs to a nation of smokers, and as his wife and daughters join him in a smoke as he journeys in the train, it does not occur to him that you, whether a lady or a gentleman, even if you don't care to smoke yourself, can derive no pleasure from the fragrance of the weed. Here let me say, *en parenthèse*, that, though the Japs are all smokers, they are none of them victims of the habit in the same sense as Europeans. The refined and delicate passion of the Japanese smoker is satisfied with two or three whiffs at a time—his diminutive pipe would not hold enough tobacco for much more—but in the course of an hour the pipe and the pouch will probably be produced again. But continuous smoking for any length of time is not the Japanese idea of indulgence in the pleasures of the weed.

On arriving at Kodzu, I left my portmanteau at a tea-house near the station in charge of two little *mousmés*, whose looks inspired me with confidence, and, after a stroll on the beach, took tram for Yumoto (about ten miles, fare 70 *sen*), with only light hand-bag. It was the longest tram ride that I had ever undertaken, and, though it was by no means monotonous, it seemed quite interminable. The road—which is the old Tôkaidô, connecting the modern with the ancient capital—led through several villages, of which the largest—Odawara—is celebrated in Japanese history as the scene of many bloody conflicts in feudal times. There is an old saying in Japan, *Odawara hyogi*, or "Odawara Conference," applied to endless talk ending in nothing. The origin of it is referred back to the sixteenth century—to an occasion when, during a siege of its castle, the defenders were prolonging the discussion of their plans, and deliberating whether they should act on the defensive or offensive, and when, during the talk, the great Hideyoshi made an unexpected attack, and took the castle by storm. The castle is now in ruins, having been finally destroyed at the time of the Revolution of 1868. Opposite its walls the tramcar changed horses, and the rest of the journey was accomplished at a brisk pace. Fuji, the Queen of Mountains, was kept in view most of the way. Arrived at Yumoto, I was met by a swarm of coolies who bore down upon me with their *rickishas*, but, instead of pushing on the same day to Miyanoshita (as is generally done), I broke the journey at a little place about half-a-mile beyond Yumoto, called Tonosawa, and spent the night at an inn—Tamano-yu—which, although the European conveniences in it were few, was nevertheless delightful. Tonosawa lies near the mouth of a gorge, and is so shut in by hills that the sun does not shine upon it for more than two or three hours a day. In all my subsequent rambles through the country, I never came upon so pleasant a *yadoya* as the Tamano-yu. Speaking of it later on in the house of a missionary, two hundred miles away, I found my host equally enthusiastic about it, and there was another reason for regarding it with special attachment in his case, as it was there that he spent his honeymoon. I was welcomed with the usual chorus of "*Ohayos*," and had no sooner sat down near the entrance than one domestic relieved me of my bag and umbrella, two others attacked my boots, like so many terriers, and, as usual, had to give up the attempt to unlace them in despair, and a fourth conducted me in my slippers to my room, along the side of a picturesque courtyard, over two or three rustic bridges spanning beautiful lakelets stocked with gold and silver fishes, through corridors glistening with polished pine and cherrywood, and, finally, up a spic-and-span stairway of cedar into a spacious chamber, innocent of furniture save two chairs, but charming in its simplicity. In a few minutes the *hibachi* (fire-box) was brought in and set in the midst, with two instruments like knitting-needles with which to stir and trim the burning fuel, and the waiting-maid, Ewa, had some excellent tea, with rice and fish, set before me, and, in accordance with the custom of the country, faced me kneeling and demurely watched me during the whole time I was at my meal. It is wonderful how soon one gets used in Japan to another looking on during one's meal, and counting, as it were, one's every mouthful. At first the guest is almost inclined to resent such attention, and to wish that the mute on-looker were in Jericho rather than in Japan; but the feeling of uneasiness soon wears away, and he becomes almost unconscious of a pair of curious, oblique, almond-shaped eyes looking on so intently. Of course the well-meaning maid knows nothing of the manners of the Far West, and, so far from meaning to be rude by staring at the stranger, does him, according to her lights, the greatest honour by assuming a position where she can at once, at the slightest sign, ascertain his orders. And if, by so doing, she can at the same time gratify a natural curiosity by watching his strange physiognomy, and his dexterity in wielding those dangerous-looking instruments—knife and fork—which probably she has never held in her dainty little hands, can you blame her? Sometimes Ewa would be joined by her sister Keo (also in service at the *yadoya*) in looking on at the wild beast feeding, and the remarks which each made to the other would probably have interested me exceedingly if I had understood them, as my person and manners were almost certainly the subject of them. Though Ewa and Keo were humble domestics at an inn, I must not omit to give them their proper titles, which would be O Ewa San ("The Hon. Miss Ewa") and O Keo San ("The Hon. Miss Keo").

After a stroll through the village, I turned in for the night, but though the bed was as comfortable as any I had in Japan—the usual *futon* on the floor—precious little sleep did I get, owing to the noise of a stream close by, and the swarm of moths, caterpillars, etc., that shared the bedroom with me. The latter evil I succeeded to some extent in mitigating. Their presence was accounted for by the *mado* (rain-shutters) having been closed before the light (electric, by the way) was turned off. The consequence was that a number of those pests, which had been attracted by the light while the room was open on two sides, were shut in, and, of course, did their level best to annoy the sleeper. Impatiently jumping out of bed, I pushed back after some difficulty the inner and outer shutters, at the risk of rousing up all in the inn, and even in the village (for in opening or closing the *mado*, you make a noise which can be heard a hundred yards off), so that my room was in the dead of night open to two of the four winds of heaven, and so it was allowed to remain a sufficient time to enable the intruders to make themselves scarce again. After closing the shutter again, and turning on the electric light, I found that the clearance had been fairly complete, and the one or two that still remained gave me little trouble. The mosquito is almost unknown at Tonosawa, but in its stead there is another little pest during July and August, a fly called *búyó*, the sting of which is said to be very painful. But I was fortunate in only knowing him by repute.

The Japs, like all Orientals, are early risers, and just as I felt that refreshing sleep, for some hours wooed in vain, was at length come on, I heard the shutters being thrown back, and the cheery "*Ohayo!*" of O Ewa San or her sister (I could not make out which) saluting me. There was nothing to be done but to be content with such sleep as I had had, and to jump into my clothes and begin the day's work. After a little more experience of native inns I found that the host and hostess were always most ready to oblige by giving orders to the servants overnight not to throw open the shutters till they had heard that the honourable guest was awake, and not to disturb his slumbers by unnecessary noise in opening other shutters of the house. But at five o'clock, in any town or village in Japan, there is such a general noise caused by the opening of shutters that the most profound sleeper cannot but be disturbed.

While my breakfast was being got ready, I sat on the balcony, admiring the beauty of the prospect at early dawn, and the strange quaintness of the scene at my feet. All the village was astir, and coolies were already trundling their *rickishas* to and from Miyanoshita. As I was squatting at my breakfast, O Ewa San took it into her little head to seat herself for a moment in the chair which I had just vacated—to her own intense amusement and that of her sister and some friends on the road below. It was evidently an attitude in which O Ewa San had not often posed.

One thing about the Tamano-yu I did not afterwards see surpassed anywhere, and that was its splendid bathroom, which contained a private tank for foreign guests. Never before had a hot water bath seemed to me such a real luxury as it did in that exquisitely fitted-up basement chamber. Everything about it was so inviting that there was a temptation to spend a longer time in the water than might perhaps be good for a foreigner's constitution. As for the natives, they can spend entire days in water of a temperature beyond the endurance of any European skin, and seem none the worse for it. Indeed, the Japs take their baths at nearly the temperature which boils an egg. And such parboiling they call refreshment! At some of the hot mineral springs there are bathers who, incredible as it may seem, spend a whole week in the water, taking their meals in it on little tables, and, when sleeping, having a stone in their laps to keep them from floating. The Jap's idea of a *dolce far niente* life is as different from the Italian's as it can be. The latter does not usually associate with it personal cleanliness, which to the average Jap, who wears his religion lightly, is perhaps even more important than godliness. It was not till I arrived in Japan that I learnt that the hotter the bath, the less likely one is to catch a chill on going out into the cold air. The European residents of Japan, though they do not parboil themselves like the natives, take a hot bath much more frequently than we do. Owing to a peculiarity of the climate, they find that hot baths suit them better than cold.

I set out early for Miyanoshita. The road was somewhat steep, but otherwise excellent. *Kurumas* were constantly passing up and down, some bearing ladies of high degree. Within a mile of the village I took a rest at a tea-house, which was perched on a spot commanding a charming view of the valley. Resuming my journey, I passed a house which had an official air about it, and in front of which squatted three natives, but the exact character of it did not strike me at the time, and I passed it at a rapid pace. Soon I heard one of the men running after me rather excitedly and shouting something which I did not quite understand. Still I went on, and still the man kept shouting to me in Japanese, till at last I heard the word "toll," when I understood at once what the commotion was about. I was, all unconsciously, evading a public toll. When the man caught me up, and said in answer to my "*ikura?*" ("how much?") in very good English, "cent and a half," I asked him, "Why didn't you bring out your English before?" He became at once speechless—his English could no further go. He had exhausted his stock— which was all that was necessary for his calling. *Murray*, that I had found so reliable, said nothing about the toll; hence what must have struck the officials as a deliberate attempt to evade it. The tax had to be paid again on the return journey in the evening,

A few minutes' further walk brought me to Miyanoshita—1400 feet above the sea—quite a little mountain village, but one of the best-known health resorts in Japan. The region is wild and picturesque, and on a commanding site facing the valley is the famous hotel Fuji-ya, which is kept in European style, and is much patronised by the foreign residents of Tôkyô and Yokohama. Another hotel, situated quite near it, is the Nara-ya, but Fuji-ya receives the larger patronage by reason of its superior accommodation, cuisine, and service.

The little mountain village is full of shops, in which are offered for sale the beautiful mosaic woodwork, and bamboo articles of various kinds, for which the region is famous. Many are the pretty walks and mountain climbs, short and long, for which Miyanoshita is the starting-point. A favourite excursion is that to Hakone, but as it required an entire day, and my time was limited, I was only able to go as far as Ashinoyu—a three miles steep mountain climb. The journey is generally done by *kago*—a species of small palanquin swung from a pole, and carried on the bare shoulders of two muscular coolies, "who trudge with a steady and firm step as though they were carrying a jackdaw in a cage instead of a burly Englishman," as a witty writer has said. The natives use much shallower *kagos*, as a rule, than foreigners, as they can double up and sit on their feet with much more dignity and comfort than ourselves. They are born of ancestors who have been sitting on their heels for more than two thousand years, and, besides being of smaller size, have not the stiff joints of the foreigner. Sometimes an arm-chair is swung on poles, in which a burly Englishman can ride with a fair degree of comfort, "like an idol in a procession."

To a good pedestrian the journey to Ashinoyu, though stiff, is not very trying. The view, as one ascends, is very striking. One eminence, Benten-yama, not far from the village, commands a magnificent panorama of the peninsula of Enoshima and Tôkyô Bay in the far distance. But the village itself has no view, as it lies in a depression, though on the summit of a mountain (2870 feet above the sea). Its immediate surroundings are bleak and uninviting.

Ashinoyu is famous for its sulphur springs, and is the resort of large numbers of Japanese, and some foreigners, who suffer from skin diseases and rheumatism. There is a semi-foreign inn (Matsuzaka-ya), which, at the time of my visit, contained a few English and German patients. One German was there with a Japanese wife, who were among my fellow-passengers the day before in the tram-car from Kodzu to Yumoto. I sat down to luncheon with them, and was much struck with their apparent affection for one another. She did not know a word of German, but he seemed to speak Japanese like a native. Doubtless her own language was a better vehicle for tender sentiments than her husband's. A French writer says of Japanese women: "Voici encore une différence, et celle-ci toute à l'honneur des jolies Japonaises! Les femmes, dans tous les pays européens, témoignent une prédilection spéciale pour une langue qui n'est pas celle de leur pays. Les Françaises parlent anglais, les Anglaises et les Russes parlent français, etc. Une Japonaise ne parle que le Japonais." That, however, is not borne out by Miss Bacon, who has written so charmingly of Japanese girls and women. Educated Japanese ladies may not show a predilection for a foreign language, but under the present system they are not the monoglots they were years ago, before Commodore Perry broke in upon the repose of old Japan. "At all higher schools," says Miss Bacon, "one foreign language is required, and often two, English ranking first in the popular estimation. Many a headache do the poor, hard-working students have over the puzzling English language, in which they have to begin at the wrong end of the book, and read across the page from left to right, instead of from top to bottom, and from right to left, as is natural to them.

After a view of Hakone and the lake from the top of the hill, I retraced my way to Tonosawa, which I reached by five o'clock, loaded with wares which form the specialty of the Hakone district. Being the only European in Tonosawa, I was regarded with a good deal of interest by the natives as I strolled about the village, and I had formed more than a nodding acquaintance with several of them when the time came for me to return. Though there is not much to see at Tonosawa itself, the picturesque situation of the little village, the kindliness of its people, the comforts of the accommodation at the Tamano-yu, and its very moderate rates, made my stay a very pleasant one. Early on Saturday I left, amid the soft *"Sayonáras"* and the invitations to " please come again " of the whole household, and took *rickisha* from Yumoto to Kodzu. Midway my coolie transferred his charge to another—a transaction to which I did not at all object, as he had seen his best days, and should long ago have been placed upon the retired list; but, though it was evident when I engaged him that he was ill-fitted for his work, I selected him out of several who offered themselves as a mere matter of charity. My new man had a far finer physique, and seemed as fresh when he suddenly drew up at Kodzu, after his five miles' run, as when he set out. The usual welcome awaited me at the tea-house, where, I need hardly say, I found my portmanteau safe and sound. After tea I took another stroll along the beach, and had gone some distance when my attention was attracted by the shouting of one of the *mousmés*, who had been sent after me to inform me that my train was due. So much uncertainty prevailed along the Tôkaidô Railway as to the arrival and departure of trains, owing to the movements of the troops, that I had been told that a train might come at any moment, or come might not come for hours. To be sure of getting the first train, one had to wait at the station, possibly for two or three hours, and that the natives very generally did, but Europeans have not their patience. While the little maid, with clattering feet, hurried on in advance to purchase my *kippu* (ticket), I rushed to see about my luggage, which, with the help of willing hands, was in a few minutes conveyed to the station, duly checked, and made ready for the van as the train steamed in. Tôkyô was reached by two o'clock.

CHAPTER VI.

TÔKYÔ.

En route to the capital—Story of Tôkyô—Area and population—Yedo—Tsukiji—Hotels—The Ginza—The Naka-dôri—The Nihon-bashi and the Megane-bashi—Shiba—Mortuary temples—Kwankôba—Uyeno—Cherry-blossoms—Museum—Christian relics—Japanese embassy to Rome—" Trampling boards "—Throne of the Mikado—Zoological Gardens—Tombs and temples—Asakusa—Colossal temple—Image of Kwannon—Pleasure and piety—Japanese English—Imperial Palace.

THE part of the line from Yokohama to the capital, which I now traversed for the first time, was built by English engineers in 1872, and was the first railway opened to traffic in the country. The journey occupies forty-five minutes, and is made by seventeen trains daily. Kanagawa (once a thriving town on the Tôkaidô), Tsurumi (surrounded by extensive rice-fields), Kawasaki (noted for a temple dedicated to Kôbô Daishi), Omori ("The Great Forest," which has almost disappeared), and Shinagawa ("River of Merchandise"), are passed in rapid succession, and the traveller arrives at Shimbashi ("The New Bridge") terminus—a modern stone structure in European style—and finds himself encircled by the busy life of one of the world's great capitals.

Before I go on to describe my own movements in this vast metropolis, and a few of the impressions with which I left it, I propose to give a few facts of interest concerning it.

Every one knows that it was formerly called Yedo, and that it is so named on the maps of our childhood. It was towards the end of 1868 that its designation was changed to Tôkyô, meaning "Eastern Capital," applied in contradistinction to Kyôtô, which means "Western Capital." It became the recognised seat of Government in March 1869. It was about 1872 that European buildings began to be erected in Tôkyô. Though the city was thrown open to visitors in 1869, it was some time later that Europeans were first allowed to reside in it. There is still only one quarter (Tsukiji) in which foreigners may lease land.

The city is popularly estimated to extend in every direction four *ri*, thus covering an area of a hundred square miles. According to the official census, the population of the whole metropolitan area is 1,628,000, but that of the city proper is not quite a million.

Tramways were laid along the main streets in 1882, electric light was introduced into the city three or four years later, and in 1890 a telephone exchange was established in it, and an electrical railway laid in one of its great public parks.

Such, in brief, has been the history of Tôkyô. That of Yedo " for the most part consists of a succession of earthquakes, fires, typhoons, epidemics, floods, and droughts" (*Murray*). In the year 1703 no less than 37,000 people are said to have lost their lives by an earthquake. An epidemic in 1773 carried off 190,000 persons. The last great earthquake occurred in 1855, when the loss of life was immense.

A great part of Tôkyô has been recovered from the sea during the last three centuries. This would include Tsukiji, the foreign concession, where—at the Métropole, situated on the Bund—I was quartered during the first few days of my stay at the capital. Other hotels in European style are the Imperial, the Tôkyô, and the Seiyo-ken.

For so vast a city, the "sights" of Tôkyô strike the visitor as being very few. Those, however, are so far apart that it takes a considerable time to make the round of them, even in the superficial manner of the English tourist. Before I had time to form any plan, I found myself on the evening of my arrival being carried by the current down the Ginza—the Broadway of Tôkyô—which has one of its ends at the Shimbashi station, and, under different names, extends in the other direction through the city for miles. Even if one is not bent upon much shopping, many an interesting hour may be spent in simply strolling down that great thoroughfare, and watching the picturesque throng of natives streaming past in holiday delight, probably the most happy people on earth. Carried along by the current, you wander at your leisure, little thinking of the *ris* and *chos* you are placing between you and your starting-point, till, if it be late at night, you have to hail a *rickisha* in order to be back at your quarters at a respectable hour. That was my experience more than once through yielding to the fascination of following the stream down that interminable thoroughfare. The Ginza is a veritable shopper's paradise, but it is as well perhaps to select your articles by daylight, and not under the glare of the lanterns and torches. The paradise of the curio-hunter is a street which runs parallel with a part of the Ginza—the Naka-dori—containing a large number of shops which look insignificant, but which are stocked with costly Japanese and Chinese curios. It is known as Curio

Street among the foreign residents. An important landmark of Tôkyô on its main artery is the Nihon-bashi ("bashi" = bridge), from which all distances in Eastern Japan are calculated. Another famous bridge, which terminates the thoroughfare, is the Megane-bashi, or "Spectacles Bridge," so called from its circular arches.

But the glories of Tôkyô are its parks, Shiba and Uyeno. There are still preserved the Mortuary Temples—marvels of Japanese art—of several of the Shôguns. That of the greatest of them all, the founder of the Tokugawa, or last dynasty—Ieyasu—is at Nikkô, as also that of his grandson, Iemitsu, and will be referred to later. For a fee of twenty-five *sen* you are conducted by the priest through the temple and mausoleum of Hidetada, the second Shôgun. The tomb is very fine, being the largest specimen of gold lacquer in the world. Each of the Mortuary Temples consists of three parts—an outer oratory, a corridor, and an inner sanctum—each rich in gold gilt, colours, and finely-carved arabesques. In feudal times, when the Shôgun came to worship the spirit of his ancestors, he alone penetrated into the sanctum, the greater *daimyôs* occupying the corridor, and the lesser the oratory.

Near the Great Gate of Shiba—famous for its

colour and elaborate carvings—is the grand bazaar of Tôkyô—the Kwankôba—where there is exposed for sale every article manufactured in Japan or required in the Japanese home.

To see Shiba—which means "grass-lawn"—aright, one should visit it in April, when the cherry-blossoms add so much to the beauty of the park. The other great park—Uyeno—is the Hyde Park and South Kensington of Tôkyô combined. In it have been held three National Industrial Exhibitions, the first in 1877, and the last in 1890. It is the most popular resort in the city, and when, in April, the cherry-blossoms are out, and all Tôkyô and his wife, in picturesque holiday attire, are there to admire them, the scene is said to be one which simply defies description. That it is a sight worth going all the way to Japan to see is admitted by the least impressionable of those who have witnessed it. Such a blending of natural beauty and quaint Far-Eastern life seems more like the work of a great painter on an immense canvas than a mundane reality. But I was not fortunate enough to witness it, and only speak of it as others have spoken of it to me; but Uyeno Park, even *minus* the cherry-blossoms, as I saw it in June, with crowds of gaily-attired natives thronging its avenues, is beautiful in the extreme.

The museum in Uyeno is one of which the country has reason to be proud. To gain even a fair idea of the contents of its various departments—technical, historical, or archæological, and those of natural history and fine art—would require several visits, and a more lengthened stay in the capital than tourists generally make. Of all the contents the national antiquities will interest the European visitor most. They include the stone arrow-heads, spear-heads, and pottery of the pre-historic period, differing but slightly from those of the West. Next come various objects, such as bells, mirrors, armour, and cooking utensils of the bronze period, and most curious of all, earthenware images of men and horses unearthed from the tumuli of great personages, where it was the practice to deposit them after the custom of burying their chief retainers alive with them had been discontinued. The department of history contains a large collection of coins, the earliest dating from the year A.D. 708, and a number of ancient manuscripts, which rank among the earliest specimens of Japanese caligraphy. In the same room are two cases, the contents of which are of pathetic interest to every Christian visitor. They are some Christian relics which have survived from the seventeenth century, when the Roman Catholic missionaries were ejected from the country, and Japan all but isolated itself from the outer world. Many of them were brought from Rome in 1620 by the embassy of Hashikura Rokuemon, who had been sent thither six years before by Date Masamune, Prince of Sendai. The official Japanese account of this embassy is at variance with the versions of it accepted by European writers. According to the former, the embassy went at the desire of the Shôgun of the day to report upon the political strength and resources of Europe, while the latter describes it what it really represented to be—a mission to recognise the Pope's supremacy. The envoy was well received at Rome, and some of the objects which he brought back and are now exhibited at Uyeno Museum remained in the possession of the Prince's family until a few years ago. Among the relics is an illuminated Latin document conferring on Hashikura the freedom of the city of Rome, a painting of him in Italian costume kneeling before a crucifix, and photographs of the Prince's letters to the Pope in Japanese and Latin. Of the same touching interest to Christians are the "trampling boards"—oblong blocks of metal or wood with figures in high relief of the Virgin and Child, Christ before Pilate, the Descent from the Cross, and other incidents of the Passion, on which people suspected of the crime of Christianity were compelled to trample by way of testifying their adjuration of the forbidden faith. The Dutch (who alone were allowed to trade with the country) are believed to have countenanced the persecution for their own selfish ends.

In other rooms are preserved some of the furniture and trappings of the courts of the Mikado and the Shôgun. The throne of the former is there, with its silk hangings which shrouded his Majesty from the gaze of ordinary mortals, who were only allowed to see his feet. There are also the State bullock cart, and a model of the State barge used by the Shôguns.

I have mentioned a few of the most interesting of the countless exhibits at the Uyeno Museum. My only regret is that, owing to Tôkyô being a city of such great distances, I was not able to visit the museum again and again. But even a cursory inspection, as mine necessarily was, is enough to stimulate one's interest in the history of the country and its unique civilisation.

In the same grounds are the Zoological Gardens of Tôkyô, which, however, are in a very embryotic state. The animal which excites the greatest interest among the native visitors is said to be an ordinary English sheep, the bleating of which terrifies onlookers, and causes them to disperse as much as would a lion's roar.

The tombs and mortuary temples of the Shôguns in Uyeno Park differ but little from those at Shiba. They are regarded as priceless legacies of the art of Old Japan, one of them being a symphony in gold and blended colours.

After a "tiffin" at the Seiyô-ken Hotel—from which I looked down upon many acres of blooming lotus—I went to see the great Buddhist temple known as the Asakusa Kwannon, so called because dedicated to Kwannon, the Goddess of Mercy. The image which is worshipped there, which is of pure gold, and has a miraculous history, is never shown, but is said to be only one and three-quarter inches in height. The disproportion between the smallness of the image and the vastness of the temple in which it is enshrined has passed into a popular saying. Instead of the image—which is too sacred to be publicly exhibited—there is produced on a certain day in the year, for the adoration of the faithful, a larger and less sacred one. Of the various other figures in the great temple, one is said to be good at curing stomach complaints, another at bringing fish into the fisherman's net, another at beautifying the complexion of the votary who strikes its face. The last has been so handled by the female faithful that its countenance has become flat and featureless. The worshipper first rings a bell, which awakens the attention of the deity, then throws a coin into a receptacle, makes his or her petition, and finally claps hands to let the divinity know that the business with him is ended. But Asakusa is not so remarkable for its diminutive idol or colossal temple as for the kind of permanent pleasure fair which goes on there, and which cannot be better described than in *Murray's* words :—

"It is the great holiday resort of the middle and lower classes, and nothing is more striking than the juxtaposition of piety and pleasure, of gorgeous altars and grotesque ex-votos, of pretty costumes and dingy dolls, the clatter of the clogs, cocks and hens and pigeons strutting about among the worshippers, children playing, soldiers smoking, believers chaffering with dealers of charms, ancient art, modern advertisements—in fine, a spectacle than which surely nothing more motley was ever witnessed within a religious edifice."

Again we are told that "the grounds of Asakusa are the quaintest and liveliest place in Tôkyô. Here are raree-shows, penny gaffs, performing monkeys, cheap photographers, street artists, jugglers, wrestlers, theatrical and other figures (*ningyô*), in painted wood and clay, vendors of toys and lollipops of every sort, and, circulating amidst all these cheap attractions, a seething crowd of busy holiday-makers."

The following is a specimen of "English as she is spoke" in Japan, copied from a public notice which caught my eye in the grounds of Asakusa.

"NOTICE!

"A wonderful show of the blood-stained garments, letters, and many other things from our officers and soldiers on the battlefield.

"The exactly resembling portraits and pictures of our military and navy excellent officers and soldiers.

"The dreadful views of battlefield with oil-painted pictures.

"Admission free."

An English notice forbidding trespassing or any other illegal act is often headed, "Kind notice," or "Very kind notice"—another proof of the innate politeness and gentleness of the people.

The Imperial Palace at Tôkyô is not open to the public, but its approaches are accessible, and are very imposing. It occupies the sight of the old castle and grounds of the Shôguns, and has been inhabited by the present Emperor since 1889. The park is enclosed by a wide moat, which, with its lotus flowers and water lilies, and myriads of wild fowl, is one of the prettiest sights in the city. The encircling wall is of enormous Cyclopean masonry.

Within are a second moat and wall, immediately enclosing the private grounds and palace of the Mikado. Miss Bacon, who was privileged to see, not only the grand reception-room, throne-room, and dining-room, but also the private apartments of the Emperor and Empress, describes the palace (in her interesting little volume on "Japanese Girls and Women") as being in Japanese style, but with various foreign additions. The larger rooms are furnished after the luxurious manner·of European palaces. The private apartments are in Japanese style, and very simple. The floors are matted, not carpeted, and the Emperor and Empress repose on them *à la japonaise*, in preference to using chairs. Their Imperial Majesties have adopted many European customs, but in their private life they still prefer the national ways.

CHAPTER VII.

TÔKYÔ (*continued*).

Bishop Edward Bickersteth's mission—St. Andrew's Church and Clergy House—Confirmation service—Eijima San—Divinity School—Lecture on the Holy Land—Mrs. Bishop—National *versus* foreign dress—Appeal by American ladies—*Plébiscite*—"Girl of the period"—National *versus* Western architecture—Old Japan in the Open Ports—Japanese *bizarrerie*—The Imperial University—Hospital—Professor Basil H. Chamberlain.

I HAD not been long in the Hotel Métropole when I was invited by the kind clergy of Bishop Edward Bickersteth's Mission in Azabu to put up at their house, of which the Rev. Armine F. King is warden. In fact, an invitation had been sent to me as soon as my arrival at Yokohama became known at the Clergy House, but the letter did not reach my quarters there till after I had set out for the Hakone Hills, and did not find me till I arrived at the port again on the eve of my leaving the country. At St. Andrew's House (as the mission-house is called), I spent a few very happy days, during which I had the opportunity of seeing a good deal of the work which is being carried on in that quarter of Tôkyô by the English clergy under the direction of Bishop Bickersteth. A church—a neat wooden structure—occupies the site of a more substantial and commodious one which was destroyed by an earthquake three years ago. I attended several of the services, both in the church and in the house chapel, and amongst them a confirmation service, at which a woman afflicted with leprosy and another suffering from an incurable disease, were candidates. That they were both suffering from an incurable disease it would be perhaps scarcely correct to say, as I have heard since that the leprous woman, Eijima San, who came direct to the confirmation from a private leper hospital, was afterwards all but completely cured by her treatment there, but, her general health having given way, she died a few months later. The bishop's apparent proficiency in the difficult language of the people whom he addressed impressed me very much. There was a good general congregation, mostly women, and it was with some difficulty that I made my way into the church through the scores of clogs—*ashidas, zoris*, and *komagetas*—that blocked the entrance. The Litany and the Preface to the Confirmation Service were read by native clergy. As the Prayer Book was in Roman characters, and not in *Hiragana*, and certain theological terms were only slightly modified from their Latin or Greek forms, I was able to some extent to follow the reading.

One of the most interesting hours that I spent at St. Andrew's was one evening when I was called upon to address the students of the Divinity School, of which the Rev. A. E. Webb is warden, on a visit to the Holy Land. At first using the simplest words that came to me, and speaking with great deliberation, I soon found that there was no need to be at such extraordinary pains to make myself understood, and that my auditory was not so deficient in knowledge of English as I had supposed. At the close, two of the scholars proposed and seconded a vote of thanks to the lecturer in faultless English.

At Bishop Bickersteth's, I had the pleasure of making the acquaintance of the well-known traveller and explorer, Mrs. Bishop (*née* Miss Bird), whose remarkable experiences, and no less remarkable power of narrating them, made her one of the most interesting personalities that I had ever met. She had only just arrived in Japan, where she is so much at home, for a short rest after an adventurous journey through Manchuria, and it was not many months before she was back again on the Asiatic continent, and travelling in the distant interior of China, to which no European had before penetrated. That a lady of so fragile a constitution as Mrs. Bishop's appears to be should have been able to bear up under such terrible sufferings as she has necessarily undergone puzzles those who come in contact with her. I was glad to be of some slight assistance to so remarkable a lady one afternoon, during my stay in Azabu, in taking a few photographic views of some of the Shiba temples.

A great question debated among educated native women at Tôkyô just now is—shall we give up our national dress and copy our European sisters? Probably ninety-nine out of every hundred English ladies who know anything of them and their country would say to them, "Don't." It is pretty well agreed among Europeans that the picturesque *kimono*, with the wide bright silk *obi*, suits the little Japanese dame far better than the foreign costume. The appeal which was made to their Japanese sisters by some leading ladies of the United States, including Mrs. Cleveland, not to abandon their own national dress, found an echo in the heart of English ladies generally interested in Japan. That appeal seems to have made a great impression upon the Japanese women, and to have complicated the difficulty which they felt in coming to a decision. As a native writer said, they "felt great pain in their bosom" how to act. For, from their own point of view, there is a great deal to be said in favour of making the change. They have the example of the Empress, who gets her dresses from Paris, and who requires all ladies appearing at court functions to be in foreign dress. Their husbands, in many cases, desire the change. It is admitted also that foreign dress allows the limbs greater freedom of movement. On the other hand, their own attire is more beautiful, more durable, much less expensive, and never goes out of fashion. A native doctor of Tôkyô has been making a *plébiscite* on the question, through the medium of a widely-circulated ladies' magazine, with the result that the national dress is pronounced to be the best, except for boys' clothing and that of business men. What is required, says the doctor, is a certain reform in the native dress, which, if carried out, would make it the best dress in the world. *Apropos* of dress, Mr. Henry Norman (who is my great authority for the above) quotes from McClatchie's translations of Japanese plays a clever and amusing description of a Japanese girl of the period. It is as follows:—

"Her figure so trim
As the willow tree's bough is as graceful and slim;
Her complexion's as white as is Fuji's hoar peak
'Neath the snows of midwinter—like damask her cheek—
With a dear little nose,
And two eyes black as sloes,
And a pair of ripe lips which, when parted, disclose
Pearly teeth—her fine eyebrows obliquely are set,
And is coiled in thick masses on top of her pate,
In a wondeful *chignon* as big as a plate:
(There are *eight* styles of *chignon*, just here I may tell
My fair readers, as known to the Japanese *belle*).
Then, to heighten the beauty bestowed on the part
Of kind Nature, she's called in th' assistance of Art,
For rice-powder to render more dazzlingly fair
Her face, hands, neck, and chin—cherry oil for her hair,
Just a *soupçon* of rouge to embellish her lip—
And a host of cosmetics my mem'ry that slip:
To complete the fair picture of bright loveliness,
Add to all this the charm of her elegant dress:
Satin, crape, and brocade,
Here contribute their aid,
For the long flowing garments in which she's arrayed,
Which hang loose from her shoulders, in fanciful fold,
All embroidered with storks and plum-blossoms in gold;
Next, a broad velvet girdle encircles her waist,
Tied behind in a huge bow—her feet are encased
In small spotless white stockings, which timidly peep
From beneath her red *jupon's* elaborate sweep;
Add a hair-pin of tortoise-shell, dainty to see;
On her brow place a circlet of gilt filigree."

One of the erroneous ideas prevalent in England

with regard to Japan, is that foreign costume is now almost the rule in that country, especially in the towns. Some English people visiting Japan expect to see on all hands "loud" tweeds, chimney-pot hats, and such Occidental innovations. On the contrary, a European dress is still a very rare exception. In Tôkyô, it would be within the mark to say that not one in a thousand wears such a dress. In the country, it is, of course, still rarer. It is almost confined to soldiers, students, police, railway and other officials, and the ladies and gentlemen connected with the Imperial Court. And even many members of the official class only wear it while on duty. At their homes they don their *kimono*, probably with a feeling of relief at being rid of a costume which Nature never intended them to wear. In the higher schools, the teachers have to wear a uniform, because the training is partly military. But even that rule is not as rigidly enforced as it once was. A highly educated Japanese has been heard to say: "The truth is we dislike Western dress. We have been temporarily using it only as certain animals take particular colours in particular seasons—*for particular reasons.*" *

The general adoption of the Western garb would

* 'Out of the East,' by Lafcadio Hearn.

necessitate quite a revolution in Japanese habits of life. Our costume is quite unsuited to a Japanese interior. The Japs still live, as they have done for thousands of years, on the floor, and it is unlikely that they will for a long time to come abandon as a nation their ancestral habits.

Another misconception with which many visitors arrive in Japan, and of which they are disabused as soon as they set foot in the country, is that the Japanese have very generally adopted Western architecture. There are, of course, foreign buildings in almost all the large towns, but they are, as a rule, confined to the foreign concessions. The exceptions would be a post-office, a railway station, a custom-house, or a factory. It is a mistake to suppose that the Open Ports have become so far Europeanised that little of Old Japan remains. You need not go into the interior to see Japanese life in its purity. On landing at Yokohama I was told that I should have to wait till I went inland before I should see native life unaffected by European influence. I saw it represented at Yokohama, and later at Kobe—not to mention Tôkyô—as faithfully as in any town far removed from Western contact. Whatever is essentially Japanese you get at the Treaty Ports and at the capital.

A French writer has recently been at some pains to bring together in a newspaper article a large number of instances of the *bizarrerie* which strikes the European observer of the Japanese and their ways, and as regards their modes of dressing he mentions the following. A European lady in evening dress makes a willing display of her neck and her arms, while her Japanese sister is careful to conceal the upper part of her body, but exposes with pride her well-formed little feet. When dressed for an evening party she is distinguished for her naked feet. A Japanese lady is richly dressed up to the age of sixteen or seventeen, while a French lady does not begin to dress till after that age. The latter tight-laces the upper part of her body, the former the lower. A Japanese Venus would be distinguished by the abundance of her clothes, and would look very grotesque to an Aryan, while the Western Venus would be regarded in Japan as a type of a very vulgar woman. We wear black as a sign of mourning, the Japanese wear white. In Europe, women of different social grades are distinguished by their toilets; in Japan, all women, from the wife of the Mikado to the simple peasant, wear the same toilet. The difference is only in the quality of the material. The European lady dreams of a lover's embraces; the Japanese lady would angrily slap on the cheek the lover (not to mention the husband) who would do anything to derange her sacred *chignon*. The European lady paints her lips and powders her face, but tries to make it pass for nature; the little Japanese dame does the same thing, but shows herself proud of her artistic embellishment, and does not try to conceal the fact that her beauty is the product of art. Why should she? Is it not *her* art? Such are a few of the numerous instances which the French journalist cites of the contrariness which differentiates Japanese ways from European.

One of the last places that I visited in Tôkyô was the Imperial University (*Teikoku Daigakko*). It stands in the extensive grounds of a former great *daimyô*. It is on the German plan, and consists of five "Colleges," namely, those of Law (including Politics), Medicine, Engineering, Literature, Science, and Agriculture. There are about 120 professors and tutors, of whom a few are foreigners. Many of the natives on the staff are graduates of some European or American university. Next to Japanese, German is the language most generally spoken at the University. In 1894 there were over 1300 students on the books. The course is four years for medicine, and three years for other subjects. All students must be graduates of one of the five higher middle schools of the country, or pass an equivalent examination at entrance. They reside either in the building or in licensed boarding-houses. They wear a special uniform, which is a cross between an English academical costume and a military dress. The discipline is semi-military, and is probably stricter than that of any university in Europe or America. Every student must provide two sureties to be responsible for his good behaviour while he is in *statu pupillari*. He has to be indoors early; he must neither drink intoxicating liquors nor smoke in his room. Whether it is the cause or the effect of the close surveillance to which he is subjected, he is said to be rather rude in his manner, especially towards foreigners, differing very much in that respect from other classes of the community. When, a few years ago, it was found necessary to impose such rigid discipline, a mutiny broke out among the students, over a hundred of whom were expelled. The University expenses, as given in the calendar, range from a maximum of 12 *yen* to a minimum of 7½ *yen* a month (about £1 10s. to about £1). That includes tuition, board and lodging, fire and light. Connected with the University, and standing in the same grounds, is a large hospital, and among other institutions, in other parts of the city, under the authority of the President of the University, are Botanical Gardens and an Observatory.

Englishmen may reflect with pride on the fact that the most distinguished member of the staff of the University is a countryman, Mr. Basil Hall Chamberlain, who is professor of Japanese and philology, and is reputed to know more of Japanese literature than any native scholar. He is one of the authors of that indispensable work, 'Murray's Handbook.'

CHAPTER VIII.

TÔKYÔ (*continued*).

Sengakuji—The Forty-seven Rônins—A Japanese vendetta—*Hara-kiri*—Grim relics—Teaching of Confucius—Meguro—The loves of Gompachi and Ko-Murasaki—Shintôist suppliants—Strange religious exercises—The water-cure for sin—"The Hundred Times"—A hallowed spot—A Japanese romance.

ONE of the most famous spots in Tôkyô is the cemetery of Sengakuji, the burial place of the Forty-seven Rônins, so celebrated in Japanese history. Though they lived less than two hundred years ago, their story reads like a romance of mythical times, and is a favourite subject of the Japanese drama. Their tombs are ranged round the sides of a small courtyard, shaded by trees, and among them is that of their liege lord, whose death they piously avenged. There is also shown a well, fenced in, over which is this inscription: "This is the well in which the head was washed; you must not wash your hands, or your feet here." In a building on the spot, called

Kanranjō, are shown, on payment of a small fee, the weapons and the armour, with other relics, of the Rônins. There are also to be seen statuettes of them carved in wood, with coloured faces and lacquered dresses. Each tomb, especially that of Oishi Kuranosuké, the leader of the band, has its tribute of water and incense laid on it by admiring pilgrims. Visiting cards also abound. When I made my own pilgrimage to the spot, I went on foot, and made my way as best I could through interminable streets with the help of a not very elaborate map. The consequence was that I had to make many inquiries, and to follow very freely the advice to "ask a p'liceman;" but though the name of the temple did not always give a clue to the place I was seeking, I found that *Shi-jū-shichi* (Forty-seven Rônins) was quickly understood. And now for the story of the famous deed, which is related fully in Mitford's 'Tales of Japan,' and which is briefly as follows.

At the beginning of the last century a powerful *daimyō*, named Asano Takumi, having made an attempt upon the life of a high court official, named Kôtsuké no Suké, by whom he had been insulted, was, in accordance with the law at the time, condemned to perform *hara-kiri* (*Anglicè*, commit suicide by disembowelling), his estate was confiscated, and his family ruined. His numerous retainers (*samurai*) were thus disbanded, and became Rônins—that is, "wave-men," tossed about, like a wave of the sea, leading a wandering and unsettled life, without ostensible means of existence. Forty-seven of them, with one Oishi Kuranosuké at their head, determined to avenge their liege lord's fate by compassing the death of Kôtsuké no Suké. They cautiously laid their murderous plans, but Kôtsuké no Suké was so jealously guarded against the danger which was suspected that there seemed no immediate prospect to the conspirators of success to their scheme. In order to throw their enemy off his guard, they dispersed and betook themselves to different employments. Their ringleader began to lead a dissolute life at Kyôto, and ultimately became so degraded that Kôtsuké no Suké, who kept a watch upon his movements, ceased to fear any danger from the old retainers of Takumi no Kami. Meanwhile Oishi Kuranosuké's associates were working in disguise at Yedo as common artisans, and, having succeeded in gaining access into Kôtsuké no Suké's house, took notes of all they saw and heard, even satisfying themselves as to who of the servants of the house were brave men, and who were cowards, and communicated all they knew to Oishi Kuranosuké, who, convinced that Kôtsuké no Suké was at length entirely off his guard, secretly left Kyôto and joined his comrades at Yedo.

It was mid-winter. One night, during a fearful storm of wind and snow, after a farewell feast together, as on the morrow they were to die, the conspirators attacked the house of Kôtsuké no Suké in two bands, killed all his fighting-men, but took Kôtsuké no Suké alive, and, in consideration of his high rank, offered him the choice of performing *hara-kiri*. This he refused to do. At last Oishi Kuranosuké, seeing that it was vain to urge his enemy to die the death of a nobleman, cut off his head, and carried it away. At dawn the band betook themselves to the temple of Sengakuji, being cheered on the way by the people in the streets, and hailed everywhere as heroes, and, on arriving at the temple-yard, washed the head of their victim in a well, and presented it as an offering before their lord's tomb. Then, while the priests of the temple read prayers, they burnt incense, and, having given all his money to the abbot, Oishi Kuranosuké addressed him thus:—

"When we forty-seven men shall have performed *hara-kiri*, I beg you to bury us decently. I rely upon your kindness. This is but a trifle that I have to offer; such as it is, let it be spent in masses for our souls!"

The abbot, with tears in his eyes, pledged himself to carry out their wishes. On the morrow they were brought before the High Court of Yedo, and, being condemned to *hara-kiri*, each met his death with heroic courage, and their corpses were buried as they had desired.

Another tomb at Sengakuji is that of a man who, in remorse for having insulted Oishi Kuranosuké when the latter lay drunk in the road at Kyôto, came to Sengakuji, and committed suicide at his grave.

Such is the story of one of the most remarkable incidents in Japanese history. The tombs and the relics of the Rônins are still highly venerated by the Japanese, pilgrimages are made to the spot from great distances, and every sixty years there is held on the spot a commemorative festival, which lasts nearly two months, and to which people flock from every quarter.

Among the relics preserved, in addition to those already named, is a receipt given by the *samurai* of Kôtsuké no Suké's son for the head of their lord's father, which the priests restored to the family

The gruesome document has been translated as follows:—

"MEMORANDUM.
 Item: One head.
 Item: One paper parcel.
The above articles are acknowledged to have been received,

Signed { SAYADA MAGOBEI.
   SAITO KUNAI.

To the priests deputed from the Temple Sengakuji:
  HIS REVERENCE SEKISHI.
  HIS REVERENCE ICHIDON."

Upon the person of each of the Rônins was a document explaining the motive which actuated them in committing the deed, and a yellow and soiled copy of it is among the exhibits. Another most interesting relic is a plan of Kôtsuké no Suké's house, which one of the Rônins secured by marrying the daughter of the designer. In all the annals of modern Nihilism or Anarchism it would be difficult to find a plot so deeply laid as was that of the Forty-seven Rônins of Japan.

The teaching of Confucius—" Thou shalt not live under the same heaven, nor tread the same earth with the enemy of thy father or lord"—was a sufficient justification of their bloodthirsty revenge. The abolition of the feudal system and the introduction of a new criminal code have done much to put an end to suicide for the sake of honour.

A favourite picnic resort—about three miles, or a little over a *ri*, out of Tôkyô—is a little village called Meguro, which is reached either by road or by the suburban railway. It is prettily situated amidst groves of feathery bamboo and an exuberance of wild flowers, but its chief attraction in the eyes of sight-seers is the burial-place of two lovers, Shirai Gompachi and Ko-Murasaki, the story of whose romantic fates is known to every reading resident of Nippon. The grave, situated near a temple, is called after the name (*hiyoku*) of a fabulous double bird (or two birds which flew with their near wings joined together) which is the emblem among the Japanese of fidelity in love. At the entrance into the village you come upon a Shintô shrine in the midst of lofty cryptomerias, which is a favourite resort of jealous women who have lost the affection of their lovers. At an early hour in the morning the suppliant betakes herself to the shrine, clad in a white *kimono*, and carrying in her left hand a little straw effigy of her faithless lover, and prays the tutelary deity to win back for her the heart of her deceiver, or else to strike him with sickness. Whether the petition is often granted is more than doubtful, but it is a superstition that has long lingered in the district, and, like all superstitions, will probably die hard. Arriving at the temple, we come, at the bottom of a stone stairway, upon a pool of clear water, fed by a small stream flowing through the mouth of a brass dragon. The spring was miraculously called into being by Jikaku Daishi, the founder of the temple, and a famous Buddhist abbot of the ninth century. A religious exercise—not unknown in other parts of Japan—is to stand naked, save the loin-cloth, under the stream for several hours, the effect of it being to wash away all sinful taint. That penitential lustration is called *Sui-Giyo*, or "water-cure" for sin, and it is to be suspected that many a light-hearted Jap exposes his naked body to the cooling stream in the warm weather from quite another motive than penitence. Many, on the other hand, are genuine devotees, and the self-sacrifice of standing beneath the stream on a bitterly cold day in mid-winter, as is often done, argues no little faith. Another religious exercise which is performed in the same precincts is the *Hiyakudo*, or "the hundred times," which consists in passing backwards and forwards between two points, repeating a prayer each time.

We are conducted to the lovers' graves, by the

merry, chattering waiting-maids of a tea-house hard by. Under a primitive pent-house in an old disused graveyard we come upon two moss-covered stones, marking the spot where lie mingled together the ashes of the two lovers. On one of the stones is this inscription: "In the old days his beauty was like that of the cherry flower, and she looked upon it with a love like that of the sunshine. These two birds have died in their too-short flight; the cherry blossoms have perished without fruit." Pilgrimages are still made from far and near to the hallowed spot, and sticks of incense burnt in memory of the steadfast love of the fair Ko-Murasaki.

The story of that love is a long one, but its outline is this.

Some two hundred and fifty years ago a handsome young retainer (*samurai*), named Shirai Gompachi, as famous for his valour and his skill in the use of arms as for his good looks, slew in a quarrel a fellow-clansman, and, becoming a *Rônin*, fled to Yedo. On his way thither he put up one night at an inn, where he found himself unwittingly among a gang of robbers. His richly-ornamented sword and dirk at once attracted their attention and excited their covetousness, and they at once planned his murder. Among the waiting-maids of the house was a beautiful damsel, fifteen years of age (which in Japan is maturity), Ko-Murasaki ("Little Wild Indigo") by name, who had beheld with a tender interest the handsome young guest. Knowing the intentions of the robbers, she went stealthily, in the dead of night, into Gompachi's room, where he was sleeping soundly after the fatigue of his flight, and, rousing him gently, told him in a whisper that the house was a den of robbers, that that night they would murder him for his sword and his clothes, and that she herself had been stolen by them from her father's house. She implored him to save himself and her. At first Gompachi was speechless, but, recovering his presence of mind, he thanked the "Little Wild Indigo" heartily, and told her that he would kill the robbers and rescue her that night. But first she was to go out of harm's way, and hide herself in a certain bamboo grove till he should join her. Accordingly she left the house that instant, and when a short time later, the thieves noiselessly opened the *shoji*, and entered the room, young Gompachi, with drawn sword, rushed upon them, and when he had cut down two, and mutilated other two, the rest escaped for their lives. Having thus rid himself of his would-be murderers, Gompachi repaired to the bamboo grove, where he found Ko-

Murasaki waiting in terror for him. Taking her by the hand, he escorted her to her home at Mikawa, and restored her to her grief-stricken parents. They were beside themselves for joy, and, in their gratitude, wished to adopt the young man as their son, and pressed him to live with them. To this Gompachi would not consent. His ambition was to attach himself to some big *daimyô* at Yedo. He promised, however, to weeping "Little Wild Indigo" that he would some day return to her, and, accepting a parting gift from her father of two hundred ounces of silver, he resumed his journey.

Before reaching Yedo Gompachi had, among various other adventures, another encounter with robbers, from whom he was rescued by one Chôbei, a wardsman, as much as by his own long sword. He became a guest at his deliverer's house at Yedo, where he lived for some months. He fell into dissolute ways, became a frequenter of the Yoshiwara, a quarter of Yedo then as now of evil repute. Soon he heard of the charms of a recent acquisition to the Yoshiwara, who already had the young bloods of the town at her feet, and he sought her out at the house where she stayed. When their eyes met they started back in astonishment, for she whose fame had spread abroad over the town was none other

I

than Ko-Murasaki, the "Little Wild Indigo" of Mikawa. In great distress she explained to him why she had been brought to that degraded position, how her parents, once so prosperous, had met with reverses, and had been reduced to great poverty, and how, to relieve them, she had followed the example of other Japanese maidens by selling herself to the master of the house where she then was, and how at last her parents had died of misery and grief. Then, with bitter tears, she appealed to him to save her again as he had done before. Her story so affected him that he vowed that he would not again forsake her. He was then too poor to purchase her liberty, but he visited her daily. At last all his money gave out; being a *Rônin* he knew not where to turn for more. In his despair, unknown to Ko-Murasaki, he betook himself to murder and robbery, and carried the money to the Yoshiwara. He continued his career of crime, murdering and plundering, till he was arrested by the authorities, found guilty, and beheaded as a common malefactor. Chôbei claimed his body and head, and buried them at Meguro. Ko-Murasaki first knew of his fate by hearing people talk of the handsome young *samurai*, whose deeds were so black that he was denied, when found guilty, the privilege of his rank, namely, death by *hara-kiri*. Overwhelmed with grief, she escaped that night out of the house, and making her way to Meguro, threw herself on the grave of her lover, where she prayed and wept bitterly. In the morning the priests of the temple found the lifeless body of the lovely "Little Wild Indigo," with a pierced throat, on the newly-made grave, and seeing what had happened, laid it side by side with Gompachi.

Such is the story of the romance which has made Meguro famous in Nippon, and has attracted, and continues to attract, thousands of natives and foreigners to the grave of the lovers, as to a hallowed spot.

Though Ko-Murasaki was a courtesan of the Yoshiwara, the priests did not consider that they were wrong in attributing to her, in the inscription on her tombstone, the virtue of *misae* (chastity). She sold herself to that life for the sake of her poverty-stricken parents, and according to Japanese ideas, especially of that age, she did not by so doing forfeit her claim to virtue. On the contrary, her self-sacrifice was deemed worthy of the highest praise.

CHAPTER IX.

NIKKÔ AND NEIGHBOURHOOD.

The Northern Railway—Unaccountable delay—"Nikkô the Magnificent"—The avenue—The Kanaya—Excessive rainfall—Divine service—The sacred bridge—General Grant—Shôdô Shônin and Shusha Daiô—Mausolea of Iyeyasu and Iyemitsu—English middies—Cascades—*En route* to Chûzenji—Images of Amida—Kôbô Daishi—The saint's calligraphy—Straw shoes—A farthing wasted—Fellow-vagrant—Japanese hill roads—Steep climb—Romantic scenery—Nantai-zan — Chûzenji — Absence of bird-life — "The Nightingale of Japan"—Senjô-ga-hara—Yumoto—Annaijô — A Japanese "interpreter"—An amusing mistake—Convivial company—Rain-bound—Return to Nikkô—Landslips—Welcomed at the Kanaya—The Lochs Katrine and Vennachar of Japan—Meeting old acquaintances—Arrival at Yokohama—American Independence Day.

ARMED with a general passport obtained from the Foreign Office of Tôkyô through the British embassy, I set out for Uyeno station (visiting the imposing Russian cathedral on the way), and took train by the Northern Railway for the famous city of temples, Nikkô, covering the intervening ninety miles in six hours. Five hours was the regular time, but the train stopped an hour at a small station as we approached our destination, but the cause "no fellow could understand." I asked in vain in such polite Japanese as I could command, and was thinking of doing the rest of the journey on foot and leaving the luggage to follow, when I saw signs that a start was at last about to be made. Nor was it a false alarm, for in a few moments we were off, and in twenty minutes drew up at Nikkô, or rather Hachi-ishi, as the station and village are called, for Nikkô, properly speaking, is the name not of a single place, but of a district. But here, as generally, by Nikkô will be meant the part of the district where stand the famous Mausolea.

The Italians say, "Vedi Napoli e poi mori" ("See Naples and then die"). Other nations have a similar saying with regard to one of their show-places. The Japs do not go so far as to say that there is nothing worth living for after you have seen Nikkô, but they assert, rather more modestly, and with a good deal of reason as well as rhyme—

"Nikkô wo minai uchi wa,
'Kekko' to iu na!"

which, being interpreted, is, "Do not use the word 'magnificent' till you have seen Nikkô." Magnificent it is admitted to be by all who have visited it, and few are the places on this earth where nature and art are seen combined in such impressive grandeur as they are at Nikkô. To lofty mountains, lovely vales, and picturesque cascades and giant forest trees are added shrines and temples whose glory is unsurpassed.

Those who do the journey by rail miss seeing to advantage one of the great attractions of Nikkô, namely, the famous avenue by which it is approached, and which is described with such eloquence by Pierre Loti in his 'Japonaiseries d'Automne.' They only get occasional glimpses of it. It leads from Utsunomiya, the junction on the Northern Railway, to Nikkô, a distance of twenty miles, and is lined throughout with the most stately cryptomerias. To see the great avenue aright, one ought to *rick'sha* its whole length; but since the advent of the railway few do so.

At Nikkô I put up at one of the most comfortable hotels of the country, the Kanaya, situated in the upper part of the village, and near the temples. One of the drawbacks of Nikkô, indeed the only drawback that I know of, is its excessive rainfall. If you are there only for a short time, the chances are that you will have to do your round of sight-seeing by dodging the showers; but in that respect Nikkô, after all, does not differ much from some of our popular Highland resorts. But if you are kept indoors by the weather more than is pleasant, the Kanaya is just one of those houses where with the usual resources you can feel comfortable at all times. I arrived on Saturday too late to begin the "lions," and as Sunday was my only entire day for Nikkô, I had to do my sight-seeing then, notwithstanding the day and a drizzling rain. An American doctor of Amoy, who had spent some weeks at Nikkô, and knew the ins and outs of the place, kindly offered to act as my guide. In the morning I held a service in the drawing-room, at the request of the proprietor, and had for a congregation a score of highly-cultivated English and American visitors, chiefly the latter, who entered heartily into the service. I and my fellow-guests deeply appreciated the proprietor's evident desire to offer his patrons all the advantages in his power, but the Kanaya, though admirably appointed in other respects, could boast no hymn-books, and so we had no singing. I hope that the deficiency will soon be supplied by some rich and generous Churchman visiting the City of Temples.

After luncheon my gentleman guide and myself set out, and in a few minutes found ourselves at the

Red Bridge, which spans the Daiya-gawa, and which, built in 1638 and last repaired in 1892, is closed to ordinary mortals, being only used by the Mikado and his family. According to my American *cicerone*, General Grant (who in the course of his tour round the world visited the Land of Gentle Manners) was offered by the Emperor the right of using the Sacred Bridge; but the plain and simple soldier would hear of no exception being made in his favour, but, cigar in mouth, crossed by the public bridge. The Sacred Bridge, which is of wood and red lacquered, rests on stone piers of great solidity fixed into the rock on each bank. It is called in Japanese "Mihashi," which means Sacred Bridge. Like everything else at Nikkô, it has its legend, which is briefly as follows. When Shôdô Shônin of pious memory first arrived at this spot, he found that owing to the steep rocks and the seething waters, his further progress was impossible. Falling on his knees he prayed fervently to the gods to come to his aid, whereupon there appeared on the opposite bank the indistinct figure of the god Shusha Daio, wearing a string of skulls round his neck, and holding in his right hand two green and red snakes, which he flung across the abyss. In an instant a bridge was seen to span the torrent "like a rainbow floating among the hills."

So impressed was the saint by the sight that he doubted the reality of the miracle, and was only convinced of the practical intervention of the god on his behalf when he saw the bridge becoming covered with long grass. Being now satisfied with the stability of the structure, he ventured upon it with his disciples, but as soon as he had reached the opposite bank, both the deity and the snake-bridge completely disappeared. Such is the legend which the Japanese relate with a sceptical smile. A shrine of Shusha Daio now marks the spot where the god appeared.

Crossing the stream and ascending through a grove of giant cryptomerias, we arrive at the great temples and tombs of the Shôguns Iyeyasu and Iyemitsu. Armed with a permit—for which we were charged 35 *sen*—we surrender ourselves to the contemplation for three hours of these matchless shrines, " as glorious in colour as the Alhambra in the days of its splendour." Each of the mausolea embraces a set of buildings every detail of which challenges the eye. The precincts include innumerable stone and bronze lanterns, portals within portals, pagodas, courts, chapels and temples and oratories, adorned with the most elaborate carvings in wood, bronze and ivory, representing gods, demons, dragons, lions, tigers, unicorns, elephants, monkeys, flowers and plants. Words can give but a faint idea of the conscientiousness of the work, the gorgeous magnificence of the whole, and the beauty of its deep green setting.

At the shrine of Ieyasu we fell in with some English middies, who had run up from Yokohama for a week-end holiday and who were nursing a grievance. They thought it "a beastly shame" that they were not allowed to have a free run of the shrine and its precincts, and chafed at the restraint placed upon them by the authorities. They probably thought it another instance of the unreasonableness of the Japanese that they were debarred from using the Sacred Bridge.

From the temples we went to see two or three of the cascades for which Nikkô is also celebrated. Their character may be inferred from some of their titles, which are Kirifuri-no-taki, or "Mist-Falling Cascade," Somen-ga-taki, or "Vermicelli Cascade" (called also Shiraito, "White Thread"), Makkura-daki, or "Pitch-dark Cascade," so-called from the possibility of passing behind the falls.

Early on Monday I left on foot for Chûzenji. Twenty minutes out of Nikkô I passed several hundred images of Amida ranged in a row on the opposite side of the Daiya-gawa, the exact number of which is said to be unknown. There is the same superstition regarding them that prevails with respect to certain Druidical stones and steeple steps in England—that they count up differently, however often they are reckoned. The natives will tell you in all seriousness, and without their habitual incredulous smile, that no two persons could number the stones alike, and that even the expedient of pasting a slip of paper on to each image as it is counted has been found to be of no avail. The largest image was some time ago carried down some distance by a flood, but was recovered and now stands at the entrance into Nikkô. Near the images is a precipitous rock in the Daiya-gawa on which is written the Sanskrit word *Hâmmam*. As the rock seems inaccessible owing to the boiling eddies, the carving of the word is ascribed to Kôbô Daishi, the famous Japanese Buddhist saint, who is said to have performed the feat by throwing his pen at the rock. But Kôbô Daishi figures so much in Japanese legend that it has been said that " had his life lasted six hundred years instead of sixty, he could hardly have graven all the images, scaled all the mountain peaks, confounded all the sceptics, wrought all the miracles, and performed all the other feats with which he is popularly credited." (*Murray*).

This eminent saint's calligraphy, though famous,

was not infallible. In a temple at Kyôtô there is shown an inscription which is ascribed to him, and one of the characters of which is faulty. This has given rise to a proverb—a Japanese rendering of the proverb that "even Homer nods"—*Kôbô mo fude no ayamari* ("Even Kôbô sometimes wrote wrong").

But after all there is nothing miraculous about the inscription in the Daiya-gawa, as there is authority for attributing it to a disciple of Jigen Daishi, only two centuries ago.

I set out from Nikkô with a pair of *waraji* (straw sandals), which are said to give a better foothold in walking along a mountainous road. They were worn tied underneath my boots, for which I had a difficulty in procuring a pair big enough, as the natives, male as well as female, have such dainty feet. In the presence of a crowd of curious onlookers, the obliging and polite little shopman who dealt in straw articles at Nikkô was at infinite pains to secure to the soles of my heavy boots the largest pair he had in stock, but, alas! I had scarcely got clear of the village when, without a warning, they flew off. Such was my first and last experience of *waraji*, which are recommended to Europeans as excellent foot-gear, but which I found of very little service. The pair cost me a farthing.

Two miles out of Nikkô I was overtaken by one of the guests of the Kanaya, Mr. Guinness of Dublin, who was touring in Japan on his way home from Burma. Leaving his *kuruma* (which was drawn by two coolies), he accompanied me on foot the rest of the stiff journey to Chûzenji. While the coolies followed the zigzag windings of the road, we ascended by the steeper short-cuts usually taken by pedestrians, arriving at a tea-house—a recognised stopping-place —halfway up the hill some time in advance of the *kuruma*. Of all hill roads perhaps those of Japan have the easiest gradient. When you have walked a mile or two up one of these roads, you are very little nearer your objective, as the stork flies, than when you set out. The extent of ground traversed is out of all proportion to the real ascent made. Hence a foot-path more or less defined cuts across these tortuous windings, and good climbers usually take the more direct and steeper way, and gain in time what they lose in comfort. *Kagos*, too, are generally taken along the shorter routes. At the tea-house we had some time for recuperating after our arduous climb while waiting for the coolies, and after another hour's effort we reached the summit, and began a gradual descent which brought us in a few minutes to the all but deserted village of Chûzenji, on the charming lake of that name. The scenery throughout was very striking, often wild and romantic. Several rugged gorges were passed, and many a cascade tempted us to linger and admire, and dominating all was Nantai-zan, the mountain monarch of that region. For quaint beauty Japanese scenery stands alone. Probably in no other country does the traveller meet with such a succession of fanciful pictures. The scenery of Nikkô and its neighbourhood represents every variety seen in the country, and no one who knows the most lovely regions of Europe and Japan would say that the following extract from the preface to a little handbook to Nikkô, compiled by an educated native, is the language of exaggerated patriotism: " I have always had a passion for travel. In my spare time I have visited new scenes and found pleasure in rambling over mountains and along the courses of rivers. I have always come back from these visits elated with pride: for I thought that the scenery of my own country was in no point inferior to that of far-famed Switzerland or Scotland." And good reason had he to be proud.

I said that Chûzenji was all but deserted. That is its normal condition. For a few days in July and August it is crowded by pilgrims who make the ascent of Nantai-zan as a religious exercise. As many as ten thousand then put up at the village. Lake Chûzenji is about 7½ miles long and 2½ miles broad, and stands 4375 feet above the sea. It was devoid of life up to 1873, in which year it began to be stocked with fish by the Government and now abounds with salmon, salmon-trout, *iwana* (a species of white trout) and other fish. My fellow-traveller and myself lunched together off salmon-trout in a *yadoya* overlooking the lake. After luncheon Mr. Guinness returned to Nikkô, while I went on 2 *ri* 27 *cho* (from six to seven miles) further to Yumoto, a little village famous for its hot springs and its picturesque position on a lake of that name. I was fortunate in making the journey from Nikkô to Yumoto at the best time of the year, when the azaleas, irises and wistarias which are common in the district were in full bloom. Two or three more beautiful cascades (one, called the Dragon's Head Cascade, being the most curious in the district) were passed, then the road led through a desolate forest, which had been ravaged by fire, and over a wide plain known as Senjô-ga-hara, or Moor of the Battle-field, so called on account of a great battle fought at the spot between the forces of Shôgun and Mikado in A.D. 1389. During such rambles one misses very much the bird life which delights the ear in the country districts of our own land. Japanese woods are oppressively quiet, but in the open country the lark, differing but little from ours, is in evidence, and during my solitary journey across the Senjô-gahara his song was always heard. Another of the feathered songsters which is sometimes heard is the *uguisu*, or "nightingale of Japan," but it has little in common with the nightingale of the West.

At Yumuto I put up at the Namma-ya, which had a full complement of guests, though I succeeded in having a "room" to myself. That was due not only to my being an Englishman, but also to my being the bearer of an *annai-jô* (or letter of recommendation) from the Kanaya at Nikkô, in which my merits as a guest were set forth in the usual hyperbolic style of Orientals, and full justice done to my supposed importance in my own country. This system of carrying a commendatory letter from one inn to another is a common one in Japan, and is a distinct advantage to European travellers. Some of the best native hotels keep printed forms of *annai-jô*, which they fill in with the traveller's name, destination, etc. In addition to a commendatory letter, the guest who has given a liberal *chadai* (tea-money) is presented on his departure with a fan or some other useful article.

No one at the Namma-ya knew a word of English,

but the landlord soon brought in, and presented to me with extravagant politeness, the landlord of a rival inn close by (the rivalry being evidently a very friendly one) as one who knew English. But, as often happens in Japan, knowledge of English in his case meant an acquaintance with a dozen English words in every-day use, which made him of very little service as an interpreter. He spent an unconscionably long time in my room, and dropped in several times afterwards before I left the village, under the idea that he was of real help to me.

Still, I had no serious difficulty in making my wants known in the house. I was becoming more and more on speaking terms with the language every day, and was congratulating myself upon the success which attended my efforts, when an amusing incident occurred which proved to me that it was one thing to cram up a stock of Japanese words, and quite another to make a right use of them. I thought I had made it abundantly plain to the *mousmé* that I wanted an egg boiled four minutes, and her "*hé! hé!*" ("yes, yes,") and "*kashikomarimashita*" (I have assented," "I have been reverential,") as she tripped out of the room to execute the order left no doubt in my mind but that my wishes were perfectly understood. It was a stunning blow to my pride at

K

my progress in the language when a few minutes later O Kikuyo San brought in, and with supreme politeness laid before me, four boiled eggs! What she must have thought of me ordering four eggs I don't know, but she seemed so anxious to make no mistake in carrying out my orders that I took the lot without comment, reserving two for the following morning. I could not scold her (my vocabulary did not include a single harsh word), and besides, in that gentle land, it is the height of "bad form" to scold the weaker sex.

I was looking forward to a good night's rest and meant to retire early, being quite "done up" after my long up-hill walk from Nikkô, but, alas! sleep till long after midnight was out of the question. In another part of the *yadoya* the native guests were so very convivial, and their hilarity was so unusually noisy, that I had to put up with the annoyance as philosophically as possible, trusting every moment to hear the party breaking up. This it did not do till the small hours of the morning. The obliging landlord would, I have no doubt, have so far deferred to the foreign guest who was lending distinction to his house as to have interfered and restrained the mirth, if he had been asked, but I was very unwilling to demand such self-sacrifice on the part of such good-tempered people who were enjoying their holiday in their own way in a popular watering-place, and who were only indulging in some innocent, if boisterous, fun. "Roars of laughter" would be no mere figure of speech, but a perfectly literal description of the general merriment. One of their number was evidently a wit. Most of the talking was done by him, and some of his sallies of humour were simply "side-splitting," judging from the screaming laughter which they provoked. However, I laid me down early on the comfortable *futon* prepared for me, trusting that the party would soon break up. But the hope was a vain one.

Yumoto is a quaint little village, and would be very pleasant but for the sulphur fumes. It is 5,000 feet above the sea, and the atmosphere in the height of summer is deliciously cool. In mid-winter, owing to the snow, the entire village is abandoned by the regular inhabitants, who migrate to Nikkô, leaving their houses in charge of a few hunters. A night and a day were to have been the extent of my stay at Yumoto, but it kept raining so incessantly that I remained there a second night, expecting every moment to see a rift in the clouds. I soon got on terms of acquaintance with all the villagers, as well as the visitors, male and female, and towards the end of my sojourn among them all seemed to know my position—that I was rain-bound and waiting till the clouds rolled by. But I spent a happy time there notwithstanding, though I looked around from time to time in vain for the silver lining. The service of the one solitary *rick'sha* of the village was repeatedly pressed upon me, but the charge was absurdly high, and I decided to hope on a little longer.

Seeing no signs of an improvement in the weather on Wednesday afternoon, and having thoroughly explored the village and its immediate surroundings, I resolved to wait no longer, and at five, amid the "*sayonáras*" of several of my newly-made friends, set out on my return journey, and reached the Kanaya by nine. I was heartily welcomed by the European visitors, who expressed surprise at what they were pleased to regard as a feat of pedestrianism. My intention on leaving Yumoto was to proceed no further than Chûzenji that night, to put up at the inn at which I had lunch on the way up, and to start for Nikkô at sunrise the following morning, in order to catch an early train for the south. Finding, however, on reaching Chûzenji that there was yet a good deal of daylight left, I decided to do the remaining nine miles that night. The visitors at the Kanaya seemed to think, too, that I had run no little risk, but, though it was a solitary journey among mountains, and much of it was done after sunset, the only real danger arose from the numerous landslips which had been caused by the heavy rains, and at more than one spot I had some difficulty in making my way in the dusk. It is commonly observed that the country roads of Japan, though well made in the first instance, are not kept in as good a state of repair as they might be. The road connecting Nikkô with Yumoto would be a very good one, and superior to most country roads in England, but for the occasional landslip or subsidence, which the authorities do not seem to think it worth while repairing. Sometimes one comes upon a large hole in the middle of the road, which it is not thought necessary to fill in or even fence in.

I have never heard the comparison made, but I should be inclined to call Lakes Chûzenji and Yumoto the Lochs Katrine and Vennachar of Japan. As I have walked the whole length of the two latter (including Achray), so I skirted nearly the entire length of the two former, and I was struck with a certain resemblance. The Japanese lakes are, of course, much higher—being veritable lakes in the clouds—but the sizes and surroundings (allowing for the peculiarities of Japanese landscape) are strikingly alike. As yet Chûzenji boasts no *Rob Roy* steamer, though it has several picturesque sampans, but there is no doubt that, as soon as it is visited by tourists in sufficiently large numbers, a dainty little steamer will be seen churning its waters. Chûzenji, like Loch Katrine, has its legends and traditions, but whether it has its Walter Scott I am unable to say.

Before quitting Nikkô the following morning, I paid a second visit to the temples, for, after all, a first visit, however thorough, can only give a confused idea of their barbaric grandeur.

On my way to the station I overtook three travel-stained natives who, radiant with smiles, hailed me as an old acquaintance. I immediately recognised them as three villagers of Yumoto, who probably had little thought of ever seeing me again.

It was night when I reached Yokohama, and on approaching the harbour I observed that the ships were illuminated and that rockets were being sent up. My fellow passengers—all natives—were much excited by the spectacle and crowded to the side of the carriage nearest the sea. It did not occur to me at first what might be the meaning of the display. That some event of great national importance—such as the birth or the accession of the Mikado, or the promulgation of the Constitution—was being celebrated I had no doubt. It was only when I thought of the date (July 4th) that it occurred to me that the Japanese might possibly be observing the American Independence Day. My surmise turned out to be correct. Not even in the States did the anniversary excite greater interest than in some parts of distant Japan. In addition to their own national holidays, the Japanese recognise also, and observe with more or less enthusiasm, Queen Victoria's birthday, the German Emperor's birthday, and the American and French national anniversaries. They are a holiday-loving people, and it matters little to them that they are celebrating the red-letter day of a country thousands of miles away.

CHAPTER X.

THE TÔKAIDÔ LINE.

Irregular service—Kindness of a Tôkyô student—Return of troops from the war—Demonstrations—"The Peerless Mountain"—The earthquake of 1891—Lake Biwa—Kobe—" Union Church "—Punkahs and fans—An Oxford Contemporary—An interesting Virginian—Cholera—Nunobiki—Rudeness of a *Mousmé*—Osaka—The castle—Captain Saris's description—The Mint—Japanese self-reliance—Kyôto—Mysterious names—Coolie *versus* donkey-boy—Story of Kyôto—" Lions " of Kyôto—Exhibition—Japan as an industrial Power—Yaami's—Return to Kobe—Arrivals from China.

I WAS kept waiting twenty-seven hours at Yokohama for a through train to Kobe. I had to go early in the day to the station to inquire, as the railway arrangements were still uncertain owing to the movements of the troops, and no reliance could be placed upon time-tables. The first available train did not leave till 10.45 that night, and at 10.30 I found myself once more on the Tôkaidô platform, surrounded by a crowd of gentle, good-natured Japs, squatting in groups, myself and a white-uniformed policeman or two alone standing. Kobe is distant from Yokohama 358 miles, and (as there are as yet no sleeping-cars on Japanese railways) the journey is a fatiguing one, and is seldom performed by tourists without a break. A "stop-over" either at Shizuoka or at Nagoya is the rule. I booked to the latter place, although it was my original intention to go on direct to Kobe. I almost dreaded a night and a day in a Japanese train. Those who had done it and survived had told me that it was about as much as poor humanity could stand. They had travelled first. Though I was going to travel second, I thought I would attempt it, but at the last moment my courage failed me and I booked to Nagoya.

Sitting opposite me in the carriage (for he actually *sat*, and did not show an irresistible tendency to tuck his feet under him and squat) was a highly intelligent student of Tôkyô, who was bound for Kyôto, and who took no little interest in his English fellow-voyager. As we approached Nagoya on Saturday morning, I did not by any means feel as if I was nearing the limit of physical endurance, and thought I might venture to carry out my original plan. Would it be necessary (I asked myself) to re-book at Nagoya? I had luggage checked to that station; how was I to have it brought along with me to Kobe? Here my friend proved of real service to me. At a busy station just before coming to Nagoya, he took my ticket with the difference in money (which he had made out from a time-table, which in Japan is also a fare-table) and the luggage-check, and in a few minutes—minutes of some anxiety to me, as I expected the train to be off every moment—he returned with a fresh ticket, having seen everything all right. The guard (or, as he called him, the "manager") under whose notice I was now brought, for the remainder of the long journey took quite a paternal interest in me, and every now and again came to the carriage window to see how I fared. Many were the kind young student's inquiries about England, and especially London, which all educated Japs hope to see before they are absorbed in Nirvâna. Train-loads of troops from the front with their kits and horses constantly passed us. At some of the stations the school-children were drawn up on the platform, in lines three or four deep, and at a signal from their teachers, as the military train steamed in, they all in unison sent up three hearty and quite British cheers. How many more thousands of the troops were to come people seemed to have no idea. For weeks several trains in the day had been entirely devoted to them, to the great inconvenience of the general public. Between Kobe and Kyôto there had been for some time only two trains a day each way, whereas ordinarily there were at least three times that number. The consequence was that those two trains were crowded like cattle-trains. When we arrived at Kyôto we found the platform literally crammed with passengers, and our long train soon proved too small, and several extra carriages had to be put on. At that season the passenger traffic between Kyôto and the neighbouring towns was abnormally heavy owing to the Exhibition, of which more anon.

For the greater part of the distance the Imperial Government Railway from the modern to the ancient capital follows the Tôkaidô, the great national highway, crossing and recrossing it at intervals. Tunnels and bridges are numerous, some of the latter of great length. Many of the rivers along the route have a bed out of all proportion to the small volume of water that generally flows down, and the bridges are consequently often very long. The bed of one river crossed—the Oigawa—is nearly a mile across, while the stream, except in flood time, is only about a hundred feet wide.

The railway passes through the broad and fertile

plain surrounding Fuji, and at Gotemba—the highest point on the line—is obtained one of the finest views of the "Peerless Mountain." Passing through the provinces of Owari and Uno, with their thickly scattered towns and villages, we see evidences still remaining of the terrible earthquake which devastated that part of the country in 1891, and by which 10,000 people perished, 20,000 were injured, and 128,000 houses were destroyed. The line runs for some miles parallel with the shore of the far-famed Lake Biwa, which is classic ground, and after passing in succession Kyôto and Osaka, we arrive at our destination.

Twenty minutes' *rickisha* ride from the station (Sannomiya) brought me to my quarters—Ballard House—patronised by missionaries and their families, and similar in its arrangements (though with stiffer charges) to Miss Brittan's at Yokohama.

Kobe (including Hyôgo), one of the five Treaty Ports and the second export city of the Empire, has a population of nearly 100,000. It has a picturesque setting, with a rugged chain of mountains as a background. It is a favourite resort, owing to the purity and dryness of its atmosphere, and its nearness to some of the most interesting places of the country. The range is dotted up the slope for some distance with fine European villas, and at night the hillside and the harbour look as if illuminated for some festive occasion. There are three foreign hotels at Kobe—the Oriental, the Hyôgo, and the Colonies. There is also a fine club with a recreation ground, upon which are played the usual English and American games, such as cricket, base-ball, lawn-tennis, etc. The main street—Moto-machi—abounds in curio shops, in which you can purchase all sorts of Japanese curiosities, from a god or goddess to a stone lantern.

The day following that of my arrival at Kobe was Sunday, and in the evening I attended service at the so-called "Union Church"—which means that it is shared by the Anglicans and the Congregationalists of the town. That evening it was the Church's turn. I am afraid that the physical discomfort which I suffered while in church interfered not a little with my profiting spiritually either by the service or the chaplain's (Rev. Sidney Swann) admirable discourse. The church was furnished with punkahs, which (although it was by no means hot) were kept going during the whole of the service. Every lady, too, had her fan, and even some of the gentlemen, for Europeans take to a fan almost as naturally as the natives, though perhaps they are not, as a rule, as graceful in the use of it. What with currents and cross currents, one worshipped at a decided disadvantage, and it was difficult to realise that we were in church at all. The multitude of fans, even without the huge punkahs, were quite enough to set up a breeze. My objection to a punkah of the sort I speak of is that you get the full force of the wind (I will not call it a cooling breeze) right on the top of the head, which, to those with a crown suggestive of a billiard ball, is not altogether pleasant. Moreover, I have known cases of a violent cold being caught from the working of punkahs, when the air was not sultry enough to require it. The operation at the "Union Church" at Kobe was, to my mind, a species of Sunday labour that might well have been dispensed with.

At Kobe I was the guest of the Rev. C. Graham Gardner and Mr. Cameron Johnson, the former a missionary of the S. P. G. and a contemporary of mine at Oxford. I was much interested in his work at Shinomiya—a quarter of the town—and in the neat little church in which he officiated to the native population. Mr. Johnson was a Virginian, and was in temporary charge of the Seamen's Mission. He was a young man of varied experience in Japan, and his account of life in the most out-of-the-way parts of the country with which he was familiar was very entertaining.

On the second Sunday it was my privilege to occupy the pulpit at the "Union Church," but the "privilege" was to a great extent discounted by the punkah nuisance. I have delivered an address with much less difficulty on an open deck in Mid-Atlantic under a stiff breeze.

The prevalence of cholera was calculated to detract from the thorough enjoyment of one's stay at Kobe, but the immunity of Europeans was to some extent reassuring. In going about the native quarter and seeing at intervals a notice on the door of a cholera-smitten house, one experienced an uneasy feeling at first, but familiarity with the sight soon deadened all sense of danger. The epidemic was supposed to have been brought from China by the troops.

Foremost among the sights of the Kobe district are the Nunobiki Waterfalls, which are about a mile from the Settlement. They consist of the Mendaki, or "Female Fall," and Ondaki, or "Male Fall." They are beautiful cascades, and large numbers of people visit them at all hours of the day, and sip tea and gossip and lounge at the tea-houses which are perched on eminences commanding the best views. *Murray* calls the tea-houses of Nunobiki noisy, and advises ladies only to go there under the escort of gentlemen. Perhaps the caution was needful. I found the *mousmés* rather more "forward" than they are in tea-houses in general. One went so far as to snatch my copy of *Murray* out of my hand, and pretended to read it to the intense amusement of her friends. It was the first act of rudeness on the part of a native that I had experienced. I have been wondering since if she knew that *Murray* did not give them a very good name. Perhaps it is scarcely likely. After the pretence of being able to read Igerisu (English), the rude little *mousmé* proceeded to examine and comment upon the sketches of gods and goddesses in the book, the names of which she gave in almost every instance correctly. The hideousness of Emma-o, of Fudo, and of the Seven Gods of Luck, seemed to cause her some amusement, as it does Europeans. In that respect probably she did not differ from less "forward" members of her race. The Japs wear their religion very lightly. They take neither life nor religion *au grand sérieux*.

From Kobe to Osaka is a journey of a little over an hour by rail. Osaka is the second city of the Empire in size, and is variously called the Venice (from its numerous bridges and canals), the Glasgow, and the Chicago of Japan. Its forest of chimney-stacks—as many as there are churches in Moscow, 368—and, generally, its commercial and industrial importance justify the latter appellations. Formerly it was the military capital of the country. According to the last census, it has a population of 361,694, and covers an area of nearly eight square miles.

One of the most important sights of Osaka is the Castle, which has played a conspicuous part in the most stirring times of Japanese history. It was built in 1583 by the great Hideyoshi, and completed in two years, the labourers being drawn from every part of the country. A magnificent palace which stood originally within the Castle no longer exists. Osaka Castle is one of those sights of Japan which stay-at-home Englishmen are apt to treat as mythical. They think that the account of it brought home by travellers must be far too highly coloured, and accordingly they make a very large mental deduction. I must confess that after all I had already seen in Japan to excite my wonder I was not altogether prepared for such a stupendous sight as Hideyoshi's fortress. I shall not attempt to add to the descriptions which have already been given of it, but content myself with quoting the quaint account of it given by the observant Captain Saris at the beginning of the

L

seventeenth century—an account which is strikingly true of the place as it appears to-day.

"We found Ozaca," says Captain Saris, "to be a very great towne, as great as London within the walls, with many faire timber bridges of a great height, seruing to pass over a riuer there as wide as the *Thames* at *London*. Some faire houses we found there but not many. It is one of the chiefe sea-ports of all *Iapan*: hauing a castle in it, maruellous large and strong, with very deepe trenches about it, and many draw-bridges, with gates plated with yron. The castle is built all of free-stone, with bulwarks and battlements, with loope holes for smal shot and arrowes, and diuers passages for to cast stones vpon the assaylants. The walls are at the least sixe or seuen yards thicke, all (as I said) of free-stone, without any filling in the inward part with trumpery, as they reported vnto me. The stones are great, of an excellent quarry, and are cut so exactly to fit the place where they are laid, that no morter is used, but onely earth cast betweene to fill vp voyd creuises if any be."

Some of the stones measure as much as forty feet in length and ten feet in height, and can only be compared to the Temple foundations at Jerusalem. Even the moats are paved with granite. The Castle now serves as headquarters for the garrison, and the prim, dapper Japanese soldier is met at every turn.

I had to obtain a permit to visit the Castle by personal application at the city office (*Osaka Fu*), where the extreme courtesy of the officials was in sharp contrast with the incivility and self-importance of many of the same class in England and America.

The same unfailing courtesy was shown to me at the Mint (*Zôhei-kyoku*), another place of interest at Osaka usually visited by foreigners. You present your card at a lodge at the entrance into the grounds (no official permit being required in this case), and in a few moments, a young man, who speaks English at least tolerably, is told off to accompany you through the building. He takes you through room after room, and explains the various stages in the process of coining with such lucidity as his knowledge of English will allow. Though he was the pink of politeness, I could not prevail upon him to allow me to carry away with me as a souvenir a silver *yen* which I had seen with my own eyes stamped and weighed, and in exchange for which I offered two *yen*. It was against the rules, and, glad as I should have been to get it, I did not press him. He volunteered the information that I could obtain any number of fresh coins at the Imperial Bank; but that was not what I wanted. I left upon him, probably, the impression that Englishmen have some curious fancies.

The Mint is now entirely worked by natives, the services of the last foreigner having been dispensed with recently. It is the same at the Government paper and printing-works at Tôkyô. A recent visitor to Japan (Mr. A. G. Boscawen, M.P.) rightly remarks in a magazine article * that, "alone of all Orientals, Japan has learnt not merely to do well under European tutelage, but to dispense with European tutelage. Other Easterns — Indians, Egyptians, Chinese — can fight and manufacture if led and organised by European officers and managers. Japan has learnt to do these things by herself. Her people have not been content to follow blindly and do what they were told, but they have gone deeper and learnt the reason why of our civilisation, and now they are applying their knowledge."

A visit to a temple or two, a stroll through the great bazaar, which, with its labyrinthine mazes, is one of the favourite haunts of the people, and a tiffin on a balcony overhanging the river Yodogawa, with its countless quaint junks, and sampans, and barges, occupied the rest of the day, and in the evening I returned to my headquarters at Kobe, again in a crowded train.

A few days later I visited Kyôto, again passing through Osaka. Though there was an event of special interest to take place that day at the Exhibition — the distribution of awards by a member of the reigning house, Prince Yamashina — the carriages

* *The National Review*, May 1896.

were not crowded, and I had a compartment almost entirely to myself. Arrived at Kyôto, I at once made for the *rickishas*, in my eagerness to be at the Exhibition in time for the Imperial ceremony, and asked a coolie to wheel me to the "exhibition," the rest of the order being in faultless Japanese. I found that the English word conveyed no meaning whatever to him. I tried "exposition," with the same result. I was soon surrounded by a swarm of coolies, to whom I repeated the name of my destination; but one and all had no idea what place I meant. How I longed for one of the donkey-boys of Egypt, who would have made out my meaning as soon as the name was uttered. If there had been an exhibition in Cairo or Alexandria, there would not have been a donkey-boy in any part of the city that would not have known the term for it in half-a-dozen languages. It is quite true that Kyôto has very little foreign element, and is not a cosmopolitan city like Cairo or Alexandria, but a considerable number of English and Americans must have run up from Kobe and elsewhere to see the exhibition. It had been open for some time, but "exhibition" and "exposition" were still terms unheard of among the *rickisha* men. I tried a railway official with a like result, and was thinking of setting out on foot to see if I could not by accident come upon the place I was seeking, when a student arrived upon the scene who at once grasped the meaning of the mysterious name—which he pronounced, as nearly as possible, "exception." Turning to the bewildered coolies, he told them that the place the "honourable English gentleman" wished to go to was the "hakarankwai." "Hakarankwai!" several of them exclaimed, looking at one another, as if each thought the others very stupid that they had not thought of it. All were now ready to take me there, and there was a keen but friendly competition for the honour. I selected the first who came up to me, and off he trundled with me merrily through two or three miles of the city, arriving just in time to be told that the ceremony was at an end. Kyôto, though not as large as Tôkyô, is yet a city of such magnificent distances, that I might have wandered about its streets for days and not come near the Hakarankwai.

The Exhibition was held in connection with the eleventh centennial celebration of the founding of Kyôto. Built by the Emperor Kwammu in 793, Kyôto was continuously the capital of the empire from its foundation till the revolution of 1868, when the Shôgunate was abolished, and the Mikado was restored to his ancestral position. It occupies an area of twenty-five square miles, and has a population of about half a million inhabitants, but since the foundation of Yedo in 1590, it has declined in size and importance. The population is only half what it is supposed to have been in mediæval times, and parts of the city which were then busy streets are now open spaces, forming parks and gardens. It is almost entirely encircled by hills, and the Tôkaidô Railway has to make a sharp bend in order to get into the city. It is a city, not of seven hills, but of thirty-six peaks, on the slopes and at the feet of which are not less than forty-five temples. Of these the Chion-In, with its bronze bell as famous as that of Moscow, the Kiomidzu, Dai-Butsu, Sanjiusangendo, and the two Hongwanjis, are among the great Buddhist shrines of the country. Well may Kyôto aspire to the ambitious title of "Rome of the Far East."

Of other buildings of historic interest at Kyôto the chief are the Imperial Palace, covering an area of nearly twenty-six acres; the Nijo Castle, with its cyclopean wall, a typical example of a Japanese fortress, within "a dream of golden beauty"; Kin-Kakuji and Gin-Kakuji—Gold Tower and Silver Tower—both monuments of the fourteenth century; Sen-yugi, for over six centuries the burial-place of the Mikados, and Kiyomizu-dera, dedicated to the Eleven-faced Thousand-handed Kwannon.

To return to the Exhibition. It was the fourth of the kind undertaken by the Imperial Government for the express purpose of stimulating progress in arts and manufactures. The charge for admission was five *sen*, equal at the then rate of exchange to $1\frac{1}{4}d$. On Saturdays it was three *sen*. For the custody of an umbrella the charge was $\frac{1}{4}d$. On a board near the entrance into the Exhibition were various notices in English as well as in Japanese, one of which, at least, is not often seen in this country, and might with advantage be placed at the entrance to our exhibitions at Earl's Court. It was this: "In case of illness within the Exhibition ground, application for medical assistance should be made to the dispensary in the western side of the Kogyo-kwan (Industrial Arts building)." Another notice ran: "No insane or intoxicated person shall be admitted, though he is provided with an admission ticket."

The main buildings were five in number, and were assigned to manufactured articles, agricultural products and implements, fishery implements, machinery, and fine art exhibits. Among the accessories were an aquarium, bazaars—where articles from all parts of the empire were exposed for sale—and tea-houses without number. To give an adequate idea of the contents of the Exhibition would require the pen of an expert. It was not as such, but as one of the masses, that I wandered for three hours through the vast buildings, admiring the splendid sample show, and lost in astonishment at the creative energy of New Japan. I was only an ordinary observer, but I could not help thinking, from the indications around me, that the day was not far distant when the Britain of the Pacific would be a formidable rival to Britain of the Atlantic.

It was said of the Tôkyô Exhibition of 1890, that to walk through all its halls and passages once meant a tramp of fourteen or fifteen miles. That of Kyôto was considerably larger. That will give a fair idea of the immense number of exhibits which had been brought together thither from different parts of the empire.

A day at Kyôto was all too brief, but it was all that could be spared. Owing to the shrinkage of the city in modern times, many of the places of interest are some distance out, and much time is spent in passing from one to another. After a hard day's sight-seeing, wound up by a good meal at Yaami's— one of the most comfortable hotels of the country, commanding a fine view of the city—I returned by a late train to my headquarters.

In the course of the day a number of English residents of Shanghai had arrived at the house, much concerned about the Chinese servants they had brought with them. They were not aware till they landed of a temporary regulation made since the war forbidding Chinese to enter the country. One family man, who had brought two *amahs*, had been to the consul and the governor, but they could do nothing for him. In the last resort he had wired to the Home Secretary at Tôkyô, the *amahs* being allowed to remain in his service pending the appeal. Whether the regulation was finally enforced I do not know, as two days later, when I left the house, no answer had been received from the Home Office. Those of the party who were visiting Kobe for the first time were quite enthusiastic over the contrast which the pleasant position of the city presented to the flat, monotonous, uninteresting environment of Shanghai.

CHAPTER XI.

KOBE AND NEIGHBOURHOOD.

Setting out for the hills—Sumiyoshi—*Kagos*—Rokko-san Pass
—Arima—Tennis-courts—The Sugimoto-ya—A Japanese
"room"—Superior *cuisine*—Complimenting the cook—
Arima wares—Departure—Escorted by a *Mousmé*—Wild
scenery—Takarazuka—Splendid hotel—"Bismarck Hill"—
Nishinomiya—School-children—Temple of Ebisu—Nara
—An interesting Persian family—Colossal image of Buddha
— Kasuga Temple — Temple of Wakamiya — Dancing
Priestesses—Temple of Ni-gwatsu-do—In love with the
Mikado—Osaka — Archdeacon Warren — Earthquakes—
Invited to re-visit Arima—Remarkable riverbeds—"Festival
of the Dead"—Suma and Akashi—Atsumori—Mr. C. E.
Fripp.

THE favourite summer resort of the Kobe residents is Arima, some nine miles from the settlement, "as the stork flies," but more like sixteen by road. It is fourteen hundred feet above the level of the sea. It is famous for its bamboo basket industry, and for its medicinal springs, which Hideyoshi is said to have used, and which are regarded as a panacea for rheumatism, and the various forms of skin disease so prevalent among the Japanese. Being difficult of access, it is not often visited by the ordinary traveller, but, though the road is rough, narrow and precipitous, to a good walker the journey is not particularly trying. There is the alternative of the *kago*, but the jolting must make that mode of locomotion along such a road scarcely less fatiguing than walking. Taking an early train to Sumiyoshi—the next station to Sannomiya—and having reduced my *impedimenta* to the smallest possible bulk—a parcel of a few pounds—I set out for the hills. Before leaving the village of Sumiyoshi, I was relieved of my parcel by an American family who were also bound for Arima, and who kindly offered to bring it along in one of their *kagos*. Walking ahead alone, I arrived in much less time than the guide-book said was necessary at the summit of the Rokko-san Pass, three thousand feet above the sea, and, looking back to admire the glorious view, saw the *kagos* about three miles down the slope, winding their way slowly like a caravan. Coolies were met at frequent intervals returning from Arima with their empty *kagos*. A journey of less than an hour down the other side brought me to the outskirts of a village, where I met an American, who, in answer to my inquiry how far I was from Arima, gave me the welcome but unexpected information that I was actually in Arima. From the top of a ridge I had made out another village, some distance beyond, to be my objective, but though the journey had not been as trying as I had heard it represented, it was trying enough, and I was not sorry at the unexpected ending of it. From the American visitor I learnt, too, that there was plenty of room in the village, though I had been told at the coast that at that time of the year—the height of the season—I should find it difficult to get accommodation. At the Sugimoto-ya, I found splendid lodging and an excellent tiffin immediately on my arrival. But I did not see Arima under the best conditions; it rained incessantly from the time of my arrival till my departure the following day. Still, I was able to take several pleasant excursions, besides rambles about the straggling village. The scenery round Arima is pretty, though not remarkable. My objection to the place as a holiday resort is that it is so shut in by mountains. That rather commends it to the Japanese, but I do not quite understand why it should be so popular with the Europeans and Americans. To the natives the chief attraction is the baths, the buildings of which are very fine.

My parcel turned up safe and sound, though some

hours after my arrival. In the course of my rambles, I was surprised, a little outside the village, to come upon two lawn tennis courts, as well rolled and limed as any I had seen elsewhere. It was not what one would have expected to see in such a distant corner of the world, but there is no "just cause or impediment" why our countrymen and countrywomen in the Far East should not have such things at their holiday resorts as well as ourselves.

My room at the Sugimoto-ya was only European in so far as it was furnished with a table and a chair, and had part of it curtained off for a bedroom, which had the luxury of a washstand, or, at least, an apology for one. There were no bedclothes proper, only the usual *futon*. The bareness of a Japanese room is never more noticed than of a rainy day, when you are obliged to be a great part of the time indoors. Then you long for the cheering look of a few homely articles of furniture. Scrupulously clean as the rooms generally are, with their artistic *kakemonos* and snow-white mats and *shoji* prettily covered with silver or gold stamped paper, the absence of furniture makes a long seclusion in them depressing. By reading and writing your mind may be diverted to some extent from your environment, but, withal, you miss the cheery aspect of an English room. But English residents who had had several years' experience of native inns and private houses told me that they did not notice it at all. They could sit or squat for hours between those bare partitions, like the natives, doing nothing but ruminating and yawning. It seemed to be their ideal of a *dolce far niente* life.

The meals at the Sugimoto-ya were so excellent that I asked on leaving to see the cook, in order to compliment her. She was entirely ignorant of English, but I had no difficulty in telling her what I wished in honorific Japanese, and, from her frequent bowing, it was evident that my language was at least intelligible; and whether it was that I was piling on the complimentary epithets too thick or not I don't know, but O Ritsu San seemed quite overcome. The native values very highly a good word from the foreigner, especially the Englishman, and will treasure it in his memory. In this case the few words of encouragement were fully deserved.

Formerly the bamboo and basket wares which are the speciality of Arima could be bought for a song, but, owing to the incursions of foreigners, prices now range from the real value of the article up to a sum many times its intrinsic worth. I did not find in Arima a ready disposition to accept less than the price originally asked for, and my "*takai*" (dear) had very little effect, but, owing to my visit being made on foot, I did not wish to encumber myself with unnecessary weight, and only carried away a few small mementoes.

I left after tiffin for Takarazuka, about eight miles distant. A *mousmé* was sent with me to the other end of the village, about a mile off, to put me on the right road. The rain held off a little during the journey. The road was an excellent one, but zigzaggy as it led down into the valley of the Mukogawa. The scenery was very wild, and the rocks more volcanic than any I had yet seen in Japan. I passed through two or three villages, at each of which I was pressed to take a *kuruma*, so rarely is a European seen walking along the route. At Takaradzuka I found a thoroughly English hotel, as comfortable as could be desired. There was nothing Japanese about it, except the mats and the maids. Perhaps I ought to add the swallows' nests, which clung to the cornices in the corridors and even in the dining-room, and to which their owners had free and unrestricted access. It was an admirably appointed hotel, and deserved a much larger patronage than it seemed to get. I found myself the only guest, and there were not many names in the visitors' book. It seemed to be patronised chiefly by Kobe residents, who went there for a week-end holiday. The situation of the hotel is very pleasant, the view of the valley of the Mukogawa from the verandah being charming. Near the hotel are some mineral baths, which are held in great repute. The village is much smaller than Arima, but is not so much hemmed in by mountains. In the neighbourhood is a hill, called by the foreign residents of Kobe "Bismarck Hill," from the resemblance of the four trees which are seen on its summit to the four hairs which the great ex-Chancellor is said to have on the top of his head. The outline also of the hill suggests the upper part of Bismarck's cranium.

On the morrow, immediately after a good English breakfast, I resumed my journey, arriving in about two hours at Nishinomiya, on the Tôkaidô Railway. The road passed through a stream with the usual wide bed, through which I had to wade, there being no bridge. In the village I met a crowd of merry-hearted children coming away from the *gakko* (school), each carrying a little umbrella and a satchel, and looking for all the world as if they had just "jumped off a fan." There was the usual gentle chorus of "*Ohayos!*" and much curious, but never offensive, gazing at the strange-looking foreigner. Japanese children are never rude—they are a model to little English barbarians as regards behaviour.

Nishinomiya is celebrated for a temple of *Ebisu*, one of the seven Gods of Luck, and the patron of honest labour. It is visited by large crowds of pilgrims on the occasion of the annual festival, which takes place in February.

From Nishinomiya I took train for Osaka, and, crossing nearly the whole of the town by *kuruma*, went by another line to Nara, where I arrived by six o'clock. I was received with much cordiality at the house of an American missionary, the Rev. Isaac Dooman, a gentleman of Persian birth, with some half-a-dozen pretty little children, whose pronounced Persian features made me think, as they ran out to greet me, that I was in the Shah's rather than the Mikado's Empire. Mr. Dooman was away in Kyôto, but Mrs. Dooman, a lady of the same nationality as her husband, showed me every hospitality. Mr. Dooman is a wonderful linguist, knowing, in addition to Persian and English (which he speaks fluently), a dozen or so other European and Asiatic languages. Mrs. Dooman, who has not the same gift of tongues, and speaks English but indifferently, interested me very much, in her broken speech, with her account of the Nestorian Christians, to which body her family belonged, several of her relatives being in the ministry. She remembered her grandfather resenting the arrival of some Methodist missionaries at Tabreez, where he lived, because they used no liturgy.

Nara was the capital of Japan from A.D. 709 till 784. Though it is supposed at present to be only about a tenth of its former size, it is a considerable place. I was informed that I was the only Englishman in the town, but not the only one of my race, as there was one American—a Congregationalist missionary.

The chief products of Nara are Indian ink, fans, toys, horns, etc.

One of the chief sights of Nara is a colossal bronze image of Buddha, which is higher by six feet than the one at Kamakura. As far as its history can be made out, it dates from the middle of the eighth century, but the present head seems to be at least the third. The first fell off about a hundred years after it was cast, and the second was melted by a fire which destroyed the building in which it stood during a civil war in 1180. The building was again burnt in 1567, and once more the head rolled off. Whether the head which it now wears is the same one restored or an entirely new one which replaced it, is not very clear. But the sight of a figure which is so venerable and which has suffered such vicissitudes has a pathetic interest even for those who do not regard it with a superstitious sentiment. It has not the calm, placid expression of that at Kamakura, being, in fact, a representation of a different deity—Roshana or Birushana—while the latter stands for Amida.

Another of the principal sights of Nara is the Kasuga Temple, which is approached by an avenue of stone lanterns, of which it is said that no one knows the exact number. The temple is of bright red, which presents a striking contrast to the deep green of the magnificent cryptomerias by which it is surrounded. In the grove are a number of tame deer, which eat out of the hands of visitors. Biscuits are sold for the purpose at the entrance. Near the main temple stands the Temple of Wakamiya, in connection with which there are in constant attendance a number of young Shintô priestesses, who, arrayed in Zouave trousers and a long gauzy mantle, and with the face plastered thickly with white-lead powder, perform an ancient dance called *kagura*. It consists of graceful figures and posturings, and is accompanied by an orchestra of three priests playing on various instruments and chanting sacred songs. The payment is a donation of at least 50 *sen* towards the service of the temple.

A fine Buddhist temple of Nara is the Nigwatsu-do, curiously built on the side of a hill, with its front and sides supported by piles, and led up to by a steep flight of stone steps. A short distance below the temple is a famous copper bell, suspended in an immense belfry, and weighing nearly thirty-seven tons. It was cast in A.D. 732.

Of a certain pathetic interest is a pretty little lake at Nara, overlooked by two fine pagodas, of which the following legend is told. In the days when Nara was the capital of the country and the abode of the Mikado, there resided at the court a beautiful maiden, whose hand was sought by all the courtiers, but who rejected their offers of marriage because she was in love with the Mikado. For a time the Emperor looked graciously upon her, but soon grew cool towards her, when she stole away from the palace by night and drowned herself in the lake.

At Osaka, on my return to Kobe, I spent a night at the house of Archdeacon Warren, through the courtesy of Mr. Meadows, who was in charge, the venerable archdeacon being away in Europe. A son —the Rev. C. F. Warren—arrived at the house shortly after me, after a long and unbroken ride from the capital. Of a certain grim interest was the drawing-room, which was wrecked by the great earthquake of 1891, when the lives of the Bishop of Exeter and others of his family were for a time in imminent peril. The room had been completely restored, and looked very little like the one which was photographed immediately after the earthquake and of which a view appears in Miss Bickersteth's book on Japan. Before retiring that night Mr. Warren kindly offered me some suggestions how to act in case of an earthquake. I was advised to rush under a doorway and remain there till the immediate danger should be over, if there should not be time to get quite clear of the building. Mr. Warren had done so only two or three days before during a shock at Tôkyô, though, as it fortunately happened, no damage was done on that occasion. One of the great drawbacks of life in that enchanted land is that you don't know what moment the house you are in may topple down, like a house of cards, about your ears. You are ever, as it were, on the brink of a volcano, and your nerves have no sooner recovered from the effects of one vibration, and you begin to forget the unpleasant sensation, than another comes to disturb your equanimity again. Though there is said to be on an average an earthquake a day in Japan, the shocks are not often such as to cause grave fears. Still, the frequency of even slight tremors gives you a disquieting sense of the insecurity of the ground under your feet, or of the roof over your head, from which we in this country are happily free.*

Notwithstanding the gruesome topic of conversation between us up to a late hour that night, my consciousness of the wreckage wrought in that very house by the terrible event of 1891, and the presence within my bed-curtain of a vicious mosquito which I had failed to evict, I slept the sleep of the just.

Mr. Warren was leaving early the following morning for Arima, and cordially invited me to accompany him and to spend a few days at his house there, where I should meet various missionaries who resorted to that popular watering-place for their holidays, but, to my regret, I was not able to spare the time for another visit to Arima.

The line between Osaka and Kobe passes through

---

* The above lines were no sooner written than the news reached England of the terrible seismic wave in Japan by which 35,000 people lost their lives.

three tunnels, which are remarkable as being under river-beds. The beds of some of the mountain torrents have been so filled up with sand and stones brought down from the hills that in many cases they have been raised some feet above the general level of the country and have the appearance of dykes. Consequently, when, as sometimes happens, a stream overflows its banks, the results are very disastrous.

When I was in the Osaka district Japan was celebrating the *Bon Matsuri*, or "Festival of the Dead." The idea of it is that the dead revisit their former earthly abodes at that season. During the anniversary cemeteries are illuminated, and white or coloured lanterns placed in the doorways of the houses—the former to guide home the disembodied spirits of those recently deceased, and the latter for the guidance of those who have left the earth for some time—and trays of rice, egg-fruit, and cucumber are placed in readiness within. The distance which the spirits have to travel is, according to the native calculation (and the Japanese have a genius for mathematics), something like 3,600,000,000 *ri*—a *ri* being about two and a half miles. The people seem to have no dread of these visitants from the spirit world: rather do they welcome them. But it is doubtful if any considerable proportion of the people really believe in what they profess to celebrate. An intelligent Japanese lady gave a striking answer to Sir Edwin Arnold who had asked her if she believed in the doctrine and in the existence of *Emma-san*, the deity of the Buddhist Hades. "You have told me before," she replied, "that *Emma-san* is only the Indian *Yama*, the Regent of the Dead, introduced into Japan; and as for the departed, who are still so dear to us, I believe they come back *kokoro no naka ni* (into the middle of our hearts), but not *taku no naka ni* (into the midst of our houses). Yet it is right to do what all the neighbours do, and to be kind to the dead if they should come; therefore I shall light my lanterns and go to say my prayers at Shiba." But whether they believe in it or not, everybody takes part in the *Bon Matsuri*.

Among other places visited in the neighbourhood of Kobe were Suma and Akashi, small seaside villages on the Sanyô line, and favourite resorts of Kobe residents. They are just at the entrance into the Inland Sea. It is remarkable that, while Japanese poets have never raved over the beauties of that far-famed sea, they have been specially enthusiastic over that part of the coast upon which stand Suma and Akashi, and which does not strike Europeans as having any particular beauty. It figures in Japanese poetry from the eighth century downward, its beauty being sung by Hitomaro, one of Japan's earliest great poets, in honour of whom there stands to-day an interesting Shintô temple at Akashi. Suma is associated in history with the death of Atsumori, the story of whose fate is the subject of a popular drama. During the Japanese struggle for political supremacy between the rival Taira and Minamoto clans in the twelfth century, Atsumori, a young nobleman of the former clan, while fleeing from battle near Suma, was about to be put to death by the veteran Kumagai Naozane under the following circumstances. When Naozane had Atsumori in his power, and had torn off his helmet with a view to cutting off his head, he was so struck with his youthful face that out of pity he hesitated to carry out his design, but, on reflecting that if spared he would ultimately fall into more ruthless hands, he decided to kill him. Atsumori submitted to his fate with heroic courage, while Naozane was so overcome with remorse that he retired to a monastery at Kyôto, and spent the rest of his days in praying for the soul of the youth whose life he had so unwillingly taken. The episode is a famous one in Japanese history and song.

Among the visitors at Ballard House was Mr.

C. E. Fripp, special artist and correspondent of *The Graphic* and *The Daily Graphic*. He had just crossed over from China, where he had made an adventurous journey, and had made some most interesting sketches, some of which he was then elaborating. A few had already appeared in the papers which he represented, and some which I saw him engaged upon I was destined to see later on in their finished excellence in those papers on my return to England. The table at Ballard House was never dull while genial Mr. Fripp was present and recounting his experiences in the Celestial Empire.

CHAPTER XII.

THE SANYÔ LINE.

Off the tourist track — Himeji — A nervous fellow-passenger — Tunnels — Okayama — The Miyoshino — *Hibachis* — Elaborate mosquito curtain—The Japanese mosquito—Disputing the bill—Honesty of innkeepers—" Tea-money " —Commercial morality of the Japanese—Japanese *versus* Chinese—The Castle and the Koraku-En—A typical Daimyô's garden—A venerable crane—The Jap as a horticulturist—Grafting—Canon Tristram—Onomichi—Extension of the Sanyô Railway—Formosa—A youthful emigrant —Hiroshima—Overrun by the military—The Mikado— *Hara-kiri*—Cholera—Heavy death-roll—Position of Hiroshima—Hospitably entertained—Visit to a sacred isle— Village demonstration—A hero of the war—Picturesque scene—Ajina—The Sampan as seen by Will Adams— Miyajima—Celebrated Shintô Temple—" Bird's Rest "— Strange religious rule—Sacred fire—Tattooing—Return to Hiroshima.

THE Sanyô line, which connects Kobe with Hiroshima, and is destined to extend as far as Shimonoseki, is seldom traversed by the ordinary tourist. Coming from the direction of the capital, he leaves the main island at Kobe, and if he travels in the contrary direction, he sets out on his land journey at the same port. But the Sanyô line, if it has not the same attractions for the sightseer as the Tôkaidô, has many features of interest, and there are several villages and towns along the route which the tourist who can afford the time would do well to visit.

But it is not to be recommended as a means of seeing the Inland Sea. You get here and there fascinating glimpses of it, but to see the glories of that famous archipelago to the best advantage, you must, of course, sail or steam through it, and that can be done either in one of the large liners which run through between Kobe and Nagasaki, or in one of the small coasting steamers which call at various ports.

The railway run from Kobe to Hiroshima takes about ten hours (distance 190 miles). At Himeji, thirty-four miles out of Kobe, you get a glimpse from the train of its ancient Castle, which is the largest in the country except that of Osaka. Founded in the fourteenth century, it was enlarged in the sixteenth by the great Hideyoshi. At Himeji (or "Himedi," as it was named on the platform), there is a station which would do credit to many a town in England of the same size. My only "stop-over" on the route was at Okayama, eighty-nine miles from Kobe, and nearly half-way. As we approached the station, we passed through a tunnel—an unusually long one for Japan, being about half a mile. When we were quite five miles off, a native, who was at the time the sole occupant with myself of the compartment, excitedly ran the whole length of the carriage, putting up all the windows, saying something to me as he darted off, the meaning of which I could only guess. I concluded that we were approaching a tunnel of exceptional length, and I expected to find ourselves in it at every moment. But as the tunnel was an unconscionably long time coming (the compartment in the meantime getting very stuffy), I was beginning to think that I had mistaken the action of my fellow-passenger, who remained throughout in a high state of excitement. When at length, after long wondering and doubting, I found myself entering a tunnel, I prepared myself for a few miles' experience of underground Japan, after the careful precaution which had been taken. After two or three minutes' absence of daylight, however, we emerged again, apparently much to the relief of my fellow-voyager, who, as soon as we were in the open air, went again the whole length of the carriage, lowering the windows. Tunnels are comparatively rare in Japan. With all its hills, a long railway journey may be made through the country without passing through a single tunnel.

Okayama lies about seven miles from the sea, with which it is connected by an excellent *jinrickisha* road. I put up at the Miyoshino inn (said by *Murray* to be near the railway station, but in reality a mile and a half away). Host, hostess, and servants prostrated themselves on their knees and noses with even greater self-abasement than I had seen anywhere else in Japan (having probably rarely had the honour of a visit from a European); but I found them one and all unusually stupid. Not only they did not know a single English word, but it was very difficult to get them to understand anything that I was not able to express in full and correct Japanese. Broken phrases, the meaning of which had been quickly grasped elsewhere, were of little use there. What they lacked in intelligence they made up in an irrepressible disposition to laughter. Except the host, who was gravity itself, they were perpetually giggling. But it was as comfortable a *yadoya* as could be wished by a weary traveller. The meals were good, and a superior *hibachi* (fire-box) was ever at my side. I don't think that I have done more than just mention once or twice this useful article, which plays so important a part in the domestic life of Japan, and which, as far as I am aware, is peculiar to that country. There are *hibachis* of all shapes and materials, but the usual one is of wood, square or oblong-shaped, and lined inside with sheet-copper. It is filled with lime-dust or sifted ashes to within an inch or two of the top, and on the heap is laid the glowing charcoal formed into a pile. Surmounting it is a small iron frame for holding the kettle, tea-pot, frying-pan, or any other kitchen utensil which may be used. The most elaborate *hibachis* have a number of little drawers and compartments where the lady of the house stows away her needles and cotton, combs, and *kanzáshis*, and are therefore workboxes and toilet-stands as well as fire-places. Some even serve the purpose of a writing-case. Then there is a special form of *hibachi*—the *tobacco-mono*—which is only used for smoking purposes, not, however, for merely lighting the pipe (*kiseru*), but for holding it and the tobacco when not in use. It is interesting to watch the mistress of the house or the serving-maid as she tends the little fire, how carefully she economizes the precious fuel, forming a miniature Fuji of the bits of charcoal, and blowing upon it till the pile is red-hot, and the kettle begins to "sing." The first thing brought to a guest at an inn or a tea-house is a *hibachi*, and even when it is not required for warmth or for lighting the *kiseru*, it is set before him as a mere matter of habit and hospitality.

At the Miyoshino I had the luxury of an elaborate mosquito curtain, which, fastened to rings at the four corners of the room, nearly filled it. It was the first I had been supplied with in a native house, and a great boon it was, as the Nippon mosquito (*ka*), bred in the paddy-fields and marshes, is one of the greatest pests of the country. Thanks to the splendid protection which I had that night, I slept soundly, but was roused unusually early by the noise of the rain-shutters (*mado*) being thrown open. There was no good remonstrating with the disturber: my Japanese was too crude to be intelligible at the Miyoshino. The curtain was speedily stripped off, and I had no alternative but to jump up and into my clothes. Here only, in all my peregrinations through the country, had I occasion to dispute the *kanjô* (bill). If I had only been slightly overcharged I should have made no fuss, but the amount was at least double what it ought to have been. There seemed little hope of getting the landlord to cut it down till a policeman happened to pass, who, on my inviting him in and showing him the account, said a few firm words to the host, with the result that a very material deduction was made. Notwithstanding the disagreement, as I mounted the *kuruma*, there was the usual chorus of "*sayonáras!*"—in which the landlord joined with apparent heartiness—and the expression of gentle good wishes for a prosperous journey. The fact is that a Japanese landlord, notwithstanding his cheery good nature and his invariable politeness, will not scruple to impose when he thinks he has a guest with whom money is no object. But give him to understand at once that you will pay the full price for all you get and even a little beyond, but that you will stand no swindling, and he will present you an honest *kanjó*. The occasional acts of gross over-charging are generally due to the idea that with the Englishman money is no object rather than to a deliberate intention to swindle. Some travellers, on arriving at an inn, hand the landlord a present (known as *chadai*, or "tea-money"), which, it is said, not only secures extra attention, but is allowed in the bill. The amount of the *chadai* varies from twenty-five *sen* to fifty *sen* per night; but it is doubtful if anything is really gained by the practice. At inns where you live entirely *à la japonaise* there is a fixed charge, known as *hatago*, which includes supper, bed, and breakfast. It varies from twenty-five to seventy-five *sen*, according to the quality of the inn and the accommodation. There is no charge for fire, light, or attendance. In some parts there is a fixed rate for accommodation only, the food being charged for according to order.

Europeans have no right to complain if they are charged at a higher scale than natives. They give much more trouble if they are unable to conform to the Japanese style of living, and if they are beyond the Treaty Ports, their host is under the obligation of reporting their arrival to the police.

Of the commercial morality of the Japs some have formed a less charitable opinion than I have expressed above. Of course I had no business dealings with them on a large scale, but some English and American merchants have spoken of them as dishonest, tricky, and altogether unscrupulous, and thought the Chinese more straightforward. The latter they credited with a good deal of the business morality as well as the business instinct of the English. The notice, said to be sometimes seen in Chinese shop-windows, and referred to in 'Sartor Resartus,' "No cheating here," is evidently an invention of the enemy.

The principal sights of Okayama are the Castle

and the Koraku-En Gardens. The former—which is shown for a small fee—is quite a museum of interesting relics illustrating the history of Japan; not all, however, relating to ancient and mediæval times, as, in addition to old swords, coats of mail, helmets, etc., I noticed guns and pistols of a generation ago. Though I found myself the sole visitor, there was a large staff of officials and hangers-on in the building, whose well-meant services in explaining to me the various exhibits were for the most part thrown away. The Gardens (Koraku-En) attached to the Castle are celebrated throughout Japan. They differ from the ordinary run of public gardens in modern Japan in being purely Japanese—with picturesque bridges, rockeries, lakes, and summer-houses—without any Western admixture. It is a typical Daimyô's garden. It is a favourite haunt of picnic parties, especially in the time of the cherry-blossoms. Four tame cranes stalk about the grounds, one of which is supposed to be two hundred years old. I naturally regarded with a great deal of curious interest so venerable a bird, whose stately gait betrayed but little his weight of years. Much of the charm of the Gardens was wanting on the occasion of my visit owing to the lakes having been temporarily drained.

Perhaps there is too much that is artificial in

Japanese gardens to be entirely pleasing to English taste. The Koraku-En was no exception to the rule in that respect. In too many ways the Jap seeks to surpass nature by art. But that he has a genius for horticulture cannot be denied. Not only does he with great success train up his children in the way they should go, but also his trees. Giant trees as well as dwarf trees are made to grow the way he would have them. The monarch of the forest no less than the young sapling has to bend to his will. Grafting is practised much more than in this country. Canon Tristram instances a full-grown maple tree with seven large branches, each having foliage of a different hue, varying from dark copper to pink and greenish white.

Two or three hours' ride brought me to Onomichi, one of the most prosperous towns in Western Japan, and a flourishing seaport. It also possesses a few fine temples, one of which—the Senkoji—is situated on the slope of a very steep hill, and is approached by a long flight of granite steps.

Up till 1894 the terminus of the Sanyô line was at Mihara, six miles beyond Onomichi. In the summer of that year it was extended to Hiroshima, which in its turn will be the terminus but a very short time, as the line is destined to end in the immediate future at Shimonoseki, and thus to connect with the Kyûshû Railway, which starts from Moji on the opposite side of the narrow straits. The section beyond Mihara runs through a hilly district, having as many tunnels probably as there are in all the rest of Japan. The country is arid and infertile, presenting a striking contrast to the other parts of the route.

Among my fellow-passengers from Onomichi to Hiroshima was a young native who was on his way out to seek his fortune in Formosa. That new acquisition of the Empire was then on the lips of every patriotic Jap, and though it had only just been taken over, and its new masters were already experiencing a foretaste of the difficulties which Li Hung Chang assured Marquis Ito they would have to cope with in reconciling the natives to the new rule, to emigrate to Formosa had already become a passion with young Japan. My youthful fellow-passenger spoke very fair English, but his account of the bright prospects before Formosa was more glowing than grammatical.

Hiroshima I found overrun by the military. It was here that the soldiers, returning from the front, first touched native soil after the hardships of the war, and the scenes at the landing-stage at the little port of Ujina—about three miles from the town—were animated and exciting. The Mikado—who made Hiroshima his residence throughout the war—frequently drove down to the port to welcome the troops. He who not many years before had been invisible to his subjects, and had ranked well nigh as a god, now showed himself openly—a plain, almost commonplace mortal in European garb—among the citizens of Hiroshima, and congratulated his faithful soldiers on their valorous deeds in the war, and spoke gracious words of welcome to them on their return.

He lived there like a private citizen, only that he worked far harder than an ordinary man, attending to affairs of state, taking his meals, and sleeping, all in one room. It is said that a rich Japanese was so filled with shame at the contrast between his own way of living and that of the Mikado at Hiroshima that he performed *hara-kiri* (*Anglicè*, committed suicide). Here I may observe, *en parenthèse*, that *hara-kiri* at the supposed call of honour is now a thing of the past, having gone with the feudal system. It was the restless, turbulent *samurai* who generally resorted to that method of avoiding disgrace, or of blotting out a stain on an honoured name. *Hara-kiri* was an honourable death. A vulgar criminal was not allowed to choose that method of leaving the world, but was despatched by the public executioner. Not to be allowed to perform *hara-kiri* was a double disgrace to a condemned *samurai*.

The "*korera-byo*," as the Japanese term Asiatic cholera, was raging at Hiroshima with even greater virulence than at Kobe, the number of deaths from the pestilence alone being one day during my visit above a hundred. There seemed to be no doubt that it had been brought from the mainland by the troops. Cholera does not seem to be endemic in Japan, as in India and other countries of the Orient. It is carried over almost every year from some part of the Continent. Notwithstanding the heavy death-roll, there was no panic, and very little to indicate the presence of so terrible a scourge. In the Far East the people have learnt by bitter experience to take such visitations with philosophic equanimity. Besides, their religion has taught them to submit with composure to the inevitable.

Hiroshima occupies a fine position at the mouth of the River Otagawa, being protected from the north by a range of hills. It is the capital of a province and the seat of a prefecture. It is a prosperous town, and resembles, though it does not approach, Osaka in the number of its canals.

I was quartered in the spacious house of the Rev. Mr. Bryan, who, like many missionaries, was spending a hard-earned holiday during the hot season among the hills of Arima. Owing to his absence I was doomed to pass the time at Hiroshima without coming in contact with a single European or American. I walked much about its intricate streets, seeing all that was thus possible of native life unaffected by European influence, but a fellow-countryman was nowhere to be seen. Still, my wants were never better ministered to than they were by Mr. Bryan's native caretaker and his wife, though the former knew but little English and the latter not a word.

From Hiroshima I made an excursion to the sacred island of Miyajima. The first part of the journey was by *ricksha* along an excellent road about ten miles to Ajina. My *ricksha*-man wore the usual hat, which has been compared to a washing-basin, a tight-fitting drawers of dark-blue cloth, with his name and number in grand characters on his back. We skirted the sea part of the way, passing through several considerable villages. We overtook a long procession of villagers—with the usual turn-

out of school-children headed by their teachers—
escorting to his home a hero of the war who had
landed that morning at Ujina. There was an
attempt at singing—probably the Japanese version
of "See the Conquering Hero Comes!" but the hero,
as usual, bore his honours with the utmost modesty,
and acknowledged with the natural gracefulness of
his race the greetings of the women and girls as he
passed. He was in the tattered uniform with which
he had gone through the campaign, and looked very
striking surrounded by men in their holiday best.

From Ajina we crossed by *sampan* the channel
(about two miles wide) separating the island from
the mainland. Owing to a strong current the
passage was made by a considerable curve, and
occupied a much longer time than might have
been expected. Meanwhile, my *kuruma-ya* lay fast
asleep, bathed in perspiration, at the bottom of the
boat, and had to be roused on our arrival at the
opposite shore.

The *sampan* seems to have changed but little
since the days of Will Adams. The description
which he gives of the mode of propelling would
apply to a great extent now. He describes the oars
as "resting vpon a pinne fastned on the toppe
of the boats side, the head of which pinne was so

let into the middle part of the oare that the oare did hang in his iust poize, so that the labour of the rower is much lesse than otherwise it must be; yet doe they make farre greater speed then our people with rowing, and performe their worke standing as ours doe sitting, so that they take the lesse roome." The old pilot's words came forcibly to my mind as I crossed the channel and watched the operation of the rowers.

Miyajima is one of the *San-kei,* or "three chief sights" of Japan in native, if not in foreign estimation, and has from ancient times been regarded as sacred. It supports a population of about three thousand, who are mainly fishermen and image-carvers. Agriculture is unknown in the island. There are several charming valleys, with the usual tea-houses commanding the most lovely views. A few deer are also found, which, as at Nara, feed out of the hands of passers-by. What gives Miyajima its sanctity is its famous Shintô temple, the *torii* of which, standing some distance out in the sea, is a favourite subject of Japanese art. The temple itself is partly built over the sea on piles. According to tradition, there was a temple at Miyajima as early as the sixth century, but owing to the destruction of the ancient archives of the island by a great fire which occurred in 1548, little is known for certain of the island before the twelfth century, when the temple had the reputation of being the most magnificent in Western Japan. Several Mikados and Shôguns, as well as a large number of powerful Daimyôs, enriched it and made pilgrimages to it from time to time. Much of it has been destroyed during the last twenty-five years, and, being of wood, the rest through neglect is hastening to decay.

The use of the *torii*, or "bird's rest," which stands at the approach to every Shintô shrine, has been a puzzle to archæologists. That of Miyajima is perhaps the most familiar to us in pictures of any. They are generally of granite, sometimes of bronze or copper. Popular shrines have often a large number of such arches leading up to them, made of fir poles painted red. Old people may sometimes be seen throwing up pebbles at the top beam in the belief that, if they lodge there, the soul of a dead relative will be benefited.

There is a religious rule, formerly more rigidly enforced than now, which forbids all deaths and births on the island of Miyajima. In the case of an unexpected birth, it is still usual to send the mother away with all speed to the mainland, where she has to remain thirty days. Though patients *in extremis* are no longer removed, all corpses are at once sent out of the island, while the chief mourners have to remain away fifty days for ceremonial purification. No dogs are allowed on the island.

On one of the highest peaks of Miyajima is preserved a sacred fire, which was lighted by Kôbô Daishi, and has never been allowed to go out.

It was late in the day when we recrossed the channel in the same *sampan*. The wind was in our teeth, and it took an hour's laborious rowing and sculling on the part of two men and a boy to get us across. The *ricksha*-man was again soon in a profound sleep, laying in a store of fresh energy for the long run which awaited him. He had thrown off nearly all his clothing, and as he lay at the bottom of the *sampan* I was interesting myself in studying the very elaborate marks which adorned his naked body. There were illustrations in red and black of birds, fishes, fans, and other objects which the Japanese love to depict, as well as various heraldic devices and symbols. Young and muscular though he was, it was not surprising that he was "dead beat" by the time we arrived at Hiroshima, as the twenty miles, all but the last one or two, had been covered at a running pace throughout.

CHAPTER XIII.

SHIKOKU.

Leaving the shores of Hondo—Impressions—Sir Edwin Arnold's 'Seas and Lands'—Shikoku—Meaning of the name—Climate—Discomfort—The passage—The Japanese born "salts"—The Mikado and Marquis Ito—Japanese dilatoriness—Hard upon the Japs—Setting out from Ujina—"First-class" accommodation—Honoured by the captain—Typhoon—Novel scene—Close scrutiny—Suspense—Mitsuga-hama—The *Ishizaki*—A miniature railway—Matsuyama—The castle—The only European in the town—The *Wayo-tei*—Reception—*Yadoya, Ryōri-ya,* and *Chaya*—A *geisha* party.

I AM about to bid "*Sayonâra*" for awhile to the shores of the Main Island, and to cross over to a separate quarter of the Empire. How shall I compress into a brief compass those impressions of strangeness and keen interest which have been crowding upon me during the six weeks I have wandered up and down this enchanted country? Sir Edwin Arnold has so beautifully described his own sensations after a few weeks' sojourn in Japan that I am tempted here to have recourse to his eloquent words and to quote them as interpreting my own feelings not less faithfully than his own. In his charming volume 'Seas and Lands' he writes as follows—

"I feel how utterly indescribable it all is, even while trying to describe this unique, unparalleled, unspoiled, astonishing, fascinating, sweet-tempered Japan. After two months spent in their midst, I have to repeat what I ventured to say after two weeks, that nowhere, for the lover of good manners, is there a country so reposeful, so full of antique grace, and soft, fair courtesies as this 'Land of the Rising Sun.' Only go among them with goodwill and sympathy, and—whatever your blunders of deportment and language—you will meet here from all ranks of the people a refinement of politeness and a charm of intercourse nowhere else experienced. I declare I have as yet never seen or heard a Japanese woman do or say anything which fell short of such a high standard of propriety, consideration, and *savoir-faire* as would be expected from a perfect English lady. If you think that is merely my ignorance or precipitancy, let me add that I am ubiquitous, and know by this time something of all classes of native society, and can still decisively recommend Japan to any public man weary with the fuss and flurry of Western life as the softest tonic, the surest restorative, the kindest and brightest panacea for too much thought and too long toil. There is not a man, woman or child within sight who ever heard of the Irish Question—think only of that! They do not know, or care to know, whence I came, and cannot even pronounce my name, because there is an 'L' in it. But because I like them they like me, and there are twenty delightful places where I can any day repair at any hour, sit on the soft white floor, sip tea, smoke, listen to the *samisen*, and hear my broken Japanese put right from the gentlest and kindest of lips and amongst ever-radiant faces. All which, I believe, is called by some the 'heathen East.'"

From Hiroshima I decided to cross over to the Island of Shikoku, of which tourists know very little. Their acquaintance with it is confined to the view which they get of its coast as they pass up or down the Inland Sea. Kyûshû in the south, and even Hokkaidô (Yeso) in the far north, are better known to European travellers than Shikoku. Except to the natives and a few missionaries, it is almost a *terra incognita*. And yet it is an island with an area equal to that of Wales. But though it is almost entirely virgin ground as far as the ordinary tourist is concerned, it is well worth visiting, and many interesting tours may be made either on foot, by *jinrickisha*, or on a pack-horse. The time at my disposal only admitted of my seeing a little of the north-western corner of the island, and I regret that I was not able to penetrate further into the interior.

The word *Shi-koku* means "four countries," the island being so called from its consisting of four provinces, Awa, Sanuki, Iyo, and Tosa. Iyo is the part to which my visit was confined. In ancient times those provinces had somewhat fanciful names, Iyo being known as "Lovely Princess," and Tosa as "Brave Youth." Their modern names are more prosaic, but the charms of Shikoku are probably not fewer now than they were in that distant age.

The climate of the island is very mild, the southern province—which is affected by the *Kuroshio*, or Japan Stream—being the only part of the Empire where two crops of rice are produced yearly. The island has several mountain ranges, ranging from 3,000 to 4,000 feet in height, and crowned by evergreen forests.

The passage from Hiroshima to Shikoku in a Japanese coasting steamer leaves much to be desired in the way of comfort. But, bad as the accommodation was, I had no right to complain, as I had been well warned what to expect. The arrangements on shipboard are so peculiarly Japanese that only those who have had considerable experience of native ways can get reconciled to them. The Japanese are born "salts." As soon as the children can even toddle, they may be seen a few yards away from land paddling their own wash-tubs. They have the spirit of the seafarer innate in them. That is not to be wondered at when we consider that they are nowhere far from the sea, and that, though the area of the country is only one-tenth larger than that of the British Isles, its coastline is more than double the length of our own.

There is a frequent service between the Main Island and Shikoku, but punctuality is rarely observed. I was down at the wharf by 4 P.M., the boat being advertised to start at 4.30, my way being through streams of soldiers and sight-seers and interminable lines of the national banner (a red sun on a white background). His Majesty the Mikado, with his great Prime Minister Count (now Marquis) Ito and other grandees, had just passed along the course, amid the acclamations of his loyal and adoring subjects. It was six o'clock before I found myself on board the little steamer, and another hour elapsed before we were off. There is not the same idea of the value of time among the Japanese as among Englishmen. In the country districts, in particular, an hour, more or less, is not of much account. It has been observed that the word *tadaima* (rendered in the dictionary "immediately," "all in good time") may mean in the mouth of a Jap any time between now and the new year. Such dilatoriness, however, must be quite exceptional. Upon the whole, for an Eastern people, they are fairly punctual. The advent of railways tends to cause them to set a higher value upon time and to acquire the habit of punctuality. The Turkish precept, "Never do anything to-day that you can possibly put off till to-morrow," is certainly not a rule of life in Japan. Though they are both an Asiatic and a squatting race, the Japs and the Turks have little in common. Mr. Boscawen seems to regard dilatoriness as a Japanese characteristic. He writes in the article from which I have already quoted of a visit to a factory, for instance, being interrupted by frequent pauses, during which he was entertained to a smoke and a cup of tea, which, though hospitable and pleasant, was a waste of valuable time. The same characteristic (he says) marked their conduct of the war. After each victory there was an unnecessary pause: "witness the long delays which occurred between the declaration of war and the battle of Ping Yang, between the latter and the taking of Port Arthur, and between the taking of Port Arthur and the attack on Wei-hai-Wei. While the Japanese commanders were, so to speak, taking a cup of tea, an European enemy would have out-manœuvred them." This is, I think, rather hard upon the poor Japs. Certainly, the writer seems to contradict himself in another part of the article, in which he says that the war was conducted in a business-like style; but he adds the qualifying clause that he was told by people who had long resided in Japan that it was the only business-like thing they had ever known the Japs do. Their management of their railways also impressed him rather less favourably than it did myself. I have already expressed my sincere admiration of their management of their railway systems, notwithstanding that I suffered some inconvenience during the dislocation of the traffic caused by the return of the troops. Mr. Boscawen, who expected the Japanese with their fifteen years' experience to do as well as the English with their fifty years' experience, says that their general management would bring discredit on "the South Eastern at its worst."

But to return from this long digression to the little craft puffing out of Ujina.

The first class was just tolerable—that is to say, one could move about to some extent, though it had to be done stooping, as the roof was only about five feet high. The occupants of the second and third classes were packed tight almost like sardines. A missionary told me that he had known the first class crammed in the same way. Fortunately it was not so when I was a passenger. I had not been long below deck, comforting myself with the reflection that things might have been worse—that there was room, at any rate, to move one's limbs, and even to lie down—when the Captain, looking in and spying an Aryan in the midst of the Mongol-Malay mass, beckoned me out and put me in his own cabin—a tiny plain room like a good-sized box, with a port-hole about the size of the pane of a policeman's bull's-eye lamp.

There was nothing to sit on, but there was the luxury of a carpet. It was an act of gentle courtesy, characteristic of Japan, towards the only European on board. When daylight disappeared, a wretched little apology for a lamp was brought in, by the flickering glimmer of which I was able with some difficulty to read. I thought it prudent to remain awake all night, as my extremities were wet from a heavy shower which came on as the passengers were on their way from the booking-office to the boat, and which gave all a good drenching. They had no sooner arrived below deck than many of them doffed some of their clothing, leaving their legs more than usually bare, and several of the ladies had thrown off their *obis* and *kimonos*.

For the first two hours we glided along pleasantly enough, but the heavy rain which came on later marred to a great extent the charms of the various islets we passed. As it was impossible to remain on deck, I had to drink in the beauty of that part of the Inland Sea through the tiny port-hole. Suddenly the boat began to get a little unsteady, and the wind to rise, though it was never more than a "capful"; and when, after an hour's slight pitching and rolling, I found that we had anchored under the shelter of an island, I learnt that there was a typhoon raging in the open sea, and that we had gone as far as it was safe to go till the storm subsided. There we remained at our moorings till some time in the morning. Notwithstanding my efforts to keep awake, I had fallen asleep on the floor of my little cabin, and when I awoke, we were again steaming ahead and approaching the other side. Before I had given up my reading in despair and thrown myself on the floor, I had taken a stroll round the other parts of the little steamer. The second class presented a strange sight enough; that of the third was like nothing so much as one's idea of the interior of a slave-dhow, except that in the former there was a little more clothing, and, of course, more cleanliness, with the absence of shackles. Perhaps also there was not quite as much huddling together, there being only one layer of humanity and parts of a second superimposed. All seemed to be in a profound slumber.

The typhoon from which we had been so well sheltered proved to have been one of exceptional violence, and wide-spread damage was done by it in Western Japan, including the wrecking of a train.

It was 9 A.M. when we arrived at the little port

of Mitsu-ga-hama, popularly known as Mitsu. Three or four other steamers and a few junks and sampans represented the shipping of the port. The effects of the terrific storm were visible all along the shore. Before we were allowed to land, a searching inquiry was made to see that we had not brought over with us from Hiroshima a case of cholera. My passport was submitted to an unusually protracted scrutiny, and some debate went on among the white-uniformed, immaculately gloved officers. I was wondering what it all meant and what it was coming to, and I was already conjuring up visions of lodgings in a house of detention, or, at least, being shipped back to Hiroshima, as generally the inspection of the passport had been very little more than a formal matter. I was beginning to think that perhaps, after all, the passport did not apply to Shikoku, or that the authorities in the island had not heard of the new regulations governing passports which had just been issued from Tôkyô, when all suspense was put an end to by one of the officers, without a word of comment and with the most engaging politeness, handing back to me the precious document. Everything proved to be all right, and my peace of mind was restored.

The landlord of the *yadoya* to which I had decided

to proceed on landing—the *Ishizaki*—was among the passengers, and had introduced himself to me early in the voyage. Escorted by him, I arrived in a few moments at his house, where I was provided with a breakfast which combined excellence with cheapness, and which was a real restorative to me in my somewhat famished condition.

Mitsu-ga-hama is the port of Matsuyama—four miles distant—with which it is connected by a miniature railway. The port having few attractions, I took an early train for Matsuyama, a boy from the *Ishizaki* seeing me off. The fare, second class, was 5 *sen*, or $1\frac{1}{4}d.$, according to the then rate of exchange. It was an interesting ride over a mountain-girt plain. There was frequent service, and the carriages were perfectly comfortable. The locomotive was scarcely as large as the "Rocket," with an American funnel.

Matsuyama is a large and bustling town, and the capital of the province of Iyo. It is dominated by a lofty hill, like an acropolis, crowned by a fine castle, formerly the stronghold of a rich and powerful Daimyô. To no other city is the Japanese word for town—*joka*—more applicable than it is to Matsuyama, for the literal meaning of *joka* is "beneath the castle." The castle dates, though not in its present shape, from the year 1603. It is a typical example of Japanese military architecture, having a keep and outer bastions. During the peaceful period of the Tokugawa Shôguns the feudal lord did not occupy his castle, but lived in a private house down in the town, surrounded by his retainers. When, in consequence of that cataclysm in Japanese politics—the downfall of the feudal system—the castles were taken over by the military department of the State, that of Matsuyama was one of the few set apart as specimens to be preserved, and treated as monuments of historic interest.

The view from the castle hill is very fine. It takes in a great part of the islet-studded Inland Sea, with countless quaint junks and fishing-boats and sampans dotting its surface, and in the dim distance the coast of Hondo, while the bird's-eye view of the large city at one's feet offers an interesting "study in roofs."

I was the only European in Matsuyama at that particular season. I called upon two American missionaries to find them gone to Arima. I had to get along as best I could with my stock of Japanese, as there seemed to be no one in the whole of that large town that could be any help to me. At least, my *kuruma-ya*, a native of the place, knew of none.

I thought that we should probably find at or near the houses of the missionaries the usual native who "knows English," but such was not in evidence.

After looking up the missionaries immediately on my arrival and finding them not at home, I was taken by my coolie to the *Wayo-tei* restaurant—a beautifully fitted-up house of a kind rare out of Tôkyô. I was greeted by the entire *personnel* of the house with the usual prostrations and a chorus of *Ohayos*, and *O ide nasai* ("Condescend to make your honourable entrance") from the cheery little hostess, and, after doffing my footgear, was conducted by a pretty, tripping *mousmé* up a shining stairway of polished cedar and pine into a long airy apartment, exquisitely panelled and matted. In Japan, I may observe here, there are three sorts of houses which accommodate travellers, namely, the *yadoya* (inn), *ryôri-ya* (restaurant), and *chaya* (tea-house). The first alone provides sleeping accommodation. The *ryôri-ya* prepares meals with less delay than the *yadoya*, while the *chaya* is a house which only provides light refreshment, such as tea and sweets. Often, however, inns are included under the general denomination of tea-houses.

While tiffin was being prepared for me at one end of the room, I was invited to join a convivial party at the other end, consisting of four young army officers and three *geisha* girls. The invitation was urged with such insistence that I had no choice but to submit. One officer came forward after another and would take no refusal, though the first sight of the company disposed me to put as much of the floor between us as possible. I was rather glad than otherwise afterwards that I had yielded to the pressure and joined the circle, as, notwithstanding a number of bottles of wine and *sakè* lying about, they did not seem to be much under the influence of drink, while I had an opportunity which cost me nothing of being present for the first time at a genuine *geisha* party.

CHAPTER XIV.

SHIKOKU.

Geisha girls—Grotesque scene—'Westward to the Far East'—
A diversion—Profession of the *geisha*—Manners rather
than morals—A French testimony—Western luxuries—
Quick-witted and stupid—Lavish attention—Excessive
heat—Novel fine—Rare luxury—Dogo—A foreigner of
importance—The charms of the Inland Sea—Canon Tristram's opinion—Ondo and Kure—All but land-locked—
Back in Hiroshima—The happiest folk in the world—
Missing a train—The philosophical natives—Special privilege—A moral—The "*korera-byo*"—A railway accident—
Fearful scene—The *Osaka Asahi*—Criticism of the native
Press—A vicious *ka*—Return to Kobe—Shinomiya—
Charms against cholera.

ENGLISH travellers generally find themselves at a *geisha* party almost as soon as they set foot on Japanese soil. It is even planned on board the boat two or three days before they sight the country, if they travel west. Passengers are asked to subscribe to a fund for getting up, as soon as they arrive at Tôkyô, a native dinner at a high-class restaurant, to the accompaniment of the music and posturing (for it is not dancing) of *geisha* girls. I had not been initiated into that phrase of Japanese life before I found myself suddenly one of such a party at the *Wayo-tei*, Matsuyama. The girls were very gaudily dressed and had most elaborate coiffures, with unusually big, fantastic *kanzáshis*, or ornamental pins. Their posturing was graceful, but the monotonous twang of the *samisen* (guitar) was anything but melody to the soul of a European. The musical part of the entertainment was of a sort that no Englishman could properly appreciate. Even the girls (whose faces were pretty enough when in repose) vied with the men in the hideousness of their expression when they attempted to sing. One of the promising youths, apparently, could not scream loud enough, or make "faces" grotesque enough, to please himself, for he seemed to strain himself so much that I had some fears that he would do himself harm. During an interval—though the *samisens* were never silent—I produced Miss Scidmore's little book 'Westward to the Far East,' the picture of the *geisha* girl in which sent the company into screams of laughter. One of the officers pointed to one of the girls as bearing a striking resemblance to the sketch, as indeed she did. The other pictures in that charmingly illustrated little hand-book also interested the merry party mightily, and I had to tell them what those sketches were which they were unable to recognise. How long the party lasted I don't know, as I left them when my tiffin was announced as ready, and there seemed no signs of its breaking up when an hour later, amid a gentle shower of *sayonáras*, I made my "honourable exit."

The profession of the *geisha* (literally, *artiste*) is not considered altogether respectable, though I observed nothing "forward" about the three at the *Wayo-tei*. They did not even share in the boisterous hilarity of their young employers, but sang and played and posed as a serious business. But *geishas* have the reputation of being frail, as well as fair. Many of them are girls with a past, as well as an ambiguous present. In their system of education manners are said to stand higher than morals. Certainly a great importance is attached to a study of the former. At the *geisha-ya*, they are trained from early youth, not only in the arts of music and dancing, but in all the etiquette of serving and entertaining guests. As to their mental equipment, I have read in a French paper that "les geishas japonaises, sorte de bayadères, sont en même temps les femmes les plus spirituelles et les plus intelligentes. Si elles savent se servir de leurs regards doux et languissants, elles savent encore davantage lancer des reparties vives et spirituelles et discuter n'importe quelle question philosophique." That is probably an exaggerated estimate of them as a class, though there may be some of them of considerable mental gifts. The same writer adds, as one of the "bizarreries" of Japan, that "chez nous, ce sont les honnêtes femmes qui brillent ordinairement par leur intelligence; au Japon, l'intelligence paraît être l'apanage des femmes menant une vie plus ou moins legère."

As I was with much discomfort squatting down in front of the raised lacquered tray which served as a table, and with no little difficulty taking my meal, it dawned upon the little landlady that a chair and a table would be just the things for me, and, motioning to me to follow her, she conducted me to a room below which had not only those two Western luxuries, but sundry others besides. In fact, I found myself, to my agreeable surprise, in a room which, but for the paper *shoji*, would be entirely European. Why she had not thought of it before is one of those things which puzzled me in my dealings with the natives. Though they are undoubtedly a quick-witted race, they sometimes show remarkable stupidity. In this particular case, my hostess may have taken me for one of those European residents of the country, who have become so habituated to native ways that they will as soon take a meal on the floor, *more Japonico*, as in the style of their native land. Perhaps it was not till she observed my painful awkwardness that it occurred to her that I was a stranger to the ways of her country. She had possibly had Europeans at her house with whom it was a matter of indifference as to whether they sat, like a Christian, or squatted, like a Buddhist or a Mohammedan. Once in the semi-European room, I was again at my ease, and had the rare advantage of being fanned while eating by two waiting-maids, assisted at intervals by the hostess, who, seeing that I was covered with perspiration (for we were in the hottest part of Japan), thoughtfully undid my collar, and sent some cooling currents down my chest. (*À propos* of the hot weather, I heard that during that summer a large firm in Tôkyô fined each one of its *employés* who complained of the heat a *sen*, because their brothers in Korea had greater heat to endure and bore it patiently. The money went to a fund for the benefit of those who were invalided home from the war.)

The meal, including the fanning and the share in the *geisha* entertainment, cost me sevenpence.

The *Wayo-tei* was a restaurant only. I slept at

an inn some distance away, to which I carried an *annai-jô* from the *Wayo-tei*. It was not, however, specially adapted for foreigners. One unusual luxury it boasted, and that was a splendid mosquito curtain of muslin, such as I had had at Okayama, against which the vicious little *ka* made vain assaults. These nets are made either large enough to cover the widest *futon* and leave a good margin, or just small enough to cover a sleeping baby. In the hot season it is a common thing to see a naked child sleeping on the floor under one of these muslin nets, which look for all the world like meat-safes.

Within a short distance of Matsuyama is a favourite watering-place of the Japanese, namely, Dôgo. Next to Kompira, famous for its ancient shrine, it is the most popular resort in Shikoku, and probably the most ancient spa in Japan. Its history extends back to the earliest times, when two gods, by bathing in its waters, gave it vogue. Subsequently five Mikados patronised it, and Dôgo became the resort of the great and the noble. It has most elaborate baths, but the supply of water is comparatively small, the flow having been to some extent interfered with by earthquakes. A speciality of Dôgo is a beautiful white faience made at a village a few miles off.

A few other short excursions were made in north-western Shikoku, till it was found necessary to return to the Main Island in order to arrive at Yokohama in time to take the home-bound steamer by which my passage had been booked.

The comforts of the native steamer were not such as to tempt me to travel in her all the way to Kobe, as might have been done. So when I returned again to the little port of Mitsu-ga-hama, I felt that a passage back to Hiroshima would be a sufficient experience of life on board a Japanese coaster.

I was taking my time over my breakfast at the *Ishizaki* when I was told that the steamer was about to start. Hurrying off, accompanied by the landlord and two or three others, I found on arriving at the wharf that the little craft was waiting for me, a messenger having, unknown to me, gone in advance to say that an important foreign personage was coming across. A sampan was in waiting at the shore to take me on to the steamer, which had already slipped her cables. Arrived on deck, still accompanied (or rather, I ought to say, attended) by the people from the inn, I was received with the ceremony befitting my supposed importance, and after wishing my Shikoku friends *sayonára* with evident regret on their side as well as my own, I set myself down to another passage across the far-famed channel. The fare was thirty-five *sen*, second class. It was not of much consequence which class I booked going back, as the passage was to be entirely by day, and, as it was beautifully fine, there would be no occasion to go below deck. As it happened, that particular boat did not carry first-class passengers. We threaded our way between islands, the channel narrowing in some parts to about a hundred yards, and we were constantly hailing villagers and half-naked brown-skinned watermen along the shore. One quaint little village, situated on the coast, seemed to have all its inhabitants at their doors greeting us as we passed. The charms of the Inland Sea baffle description. At ever turn of the bow I was fascinated by some new picture. It appears that there are some people who have been disappointed in the Inland Sea, just as there are some who thought Niagara a "fraud." I don't know what such peculiar people went out to see, but, for my part, I agree entirely with Canon Tristram, who believes it to be "for beauty and loveliness, absolutely without a rival in the world. I do not say this hastily (continues the same writer), for I had the good fortune to make the voyage three times—twice from south to north, and once the return voyage—and these were so timed that on one or other occasion I have traversed every mile of that fairy sea in full sunlight. Let the traveller recall the finest bits of coast scenery he can recollect—the Bay of Naples in spring, Wemyss Bay on a summer's morning, a trip round the Isle of Wight, threading the islands of Denmark's Sounds, the luxuriance of the Sumatran coast, the windings of the coral islets of Bermuda—recall whichever of them you please, wait but an hour or two, and you will match it in the Inland Sea." I saw very little of it compared with Canon Tristram, but I crossed it twice at one of its most lovely parts, and, having seen some of the finest coast sceneries of the world, I do not hesitate to say that, as far as my knowledge goes, the Inland Sea stands alone.

We stopped at two villages—Ondo and Kure—to pick up passengers, and to land and take on mail-bags. The shore near the former was lined with sampans. Off the latter was a fine Japanese ironclad and two large merchant steamers. I afterwards found that it was an important naval station. Near it is the island of Etajima, on which is situated the Imperial Naval College, containing a large number of cadets. More than once I found myself surrounded by land, with apparently no possible way of getting out. When I was satisfied in my own mind that we were completely land-locked, and there was not the shadow of a doubt about it, an extraordinarily narrow passage would begin to appear, through which the little steamer had to proceed with the utmost wariness to avoid disaster. We arrived at Ujina much earlier than I expected. The passage, notwithstanding the poor accommodation, had been so replete with interest that the time had passed away all too quickly. Hiroshima presented the same gay appearance as when I passed through on my journey out. The road leading from the port was thronged with the cheery, chattering and friendly little folk I had known all my life on fans and screens and lacquered tea-trays. Mingled with the military, they seemed the most good-tempered little people in the world. It was with difficulty that my *rickisha*-man succeeded in trundling his machine through without falling foul of one of the merry throng.

The following morning I was at the station by ten, intending to take the only train that ran through to Kobe in a day, which was timed to leave at 10.30. In England, if you are at a station half an hour before time, you feel pretty sure of your train. Not so, however, in the Far East. I found the approach to the booking-office thronged with people. I duly placed myself at the tail end of a line of natives waiting to be booked, some thirty yards long. At

10.15 the booking began, and when I was within a few feet of the booking place, I had the mortification of hearing it closed, and, a moment later, of seeing the train start. Though by this time I had a score of others to the rear of me, I was probably the only one of those left behind that was particularly put out by the occurrence. The rest seemed to take it with the greatest unconcern, and dispersed without a murmur, some to the waiting-room to gossip and read their *Nichi Nichi Shimbun* ("Daily News"), and others to a tea-house over the way, to while away as best they could the three hours' interval before the next train, trusting to better luck next time. Time was no object with them. As for myself, I cannot say that I was quite as philosophical under it all, and I was, I fear, more forcible than polite in my speech to the clerk when I managed to get at him. But my wrath was partially appeased when I understood from him that if he had known that there was an English gentleman in the line, and that he was bound through for Kobe, he would have booked him at once. Then I remembered that my *rickisha*-man, when he brought me up to the station, seemed inclined to take me into the booking-office, regardless of the long array of people stretching out beyond the precincts of the station, when I paid him off took my place, as the last arrival, at the tail end to await my turn. I could not see that I had any right to be booked before others who were there before me, and I did not wish to take advantage of the kind and courteous nature of the people among whom I found myself; but it turned out that I had some sort of a right, and that it was recognised by the officials. I mention the incident for the warning of any of my readers who may find themselves similarly situated in Japan. The moral of it is, that if you are at a railway station in a crowd, even half an hour before your train, and are backward in going forward to be booked, you will be left behind, as I was left before.

The next train left at 1.30, and I was glad to get away by it and out of the atmosphere of Hiroshima, where the word "*korera-byo*" (cholera) constantly fell upon my ears, though the train only took me as far as Okayama, which was reached at 8.30. As we approached Onomichi we came upon a scene almost without a parallel in England—netted with railways as it is—in the annals of its railway accidents. It was the wreck of a train which had been hurled over an embankment into the sea a short time before. The train was a special one despatched from Hiroshima with nearly four hundred sick and wounded soldiers. Near a village called Kihara, a few miles from Onomichi, the ballast of an embankment which ran along the shore had been washed away by the typhoon. Of twenty-three cars and two locomotives (one in front and the other in the rear) forming the train, the front engine and twelve cars rushed over the embankment and into the surf. It was one o'clock in the morning and very dark. Five carriages were smashed to pieces. The locomotive disappeared in the sand, the driver and stoker going with it. The killed and injured exceeded a hundred. As our train approached the spot, I noticed an unusual excitement among the passengers. I thought at first that it was caused by our approaching a tunnel, but there was no general closing of windows, which the Japanese are so particular about doing. At last they all made a rush for the side of the carriage nearest the sea. Just as it was dawning upon me that a railway accident had occurred, we came in full sight of the wreckage. It was a fearful scene, but we saw it but a few moments, as our train passed slowly along and did not stop, the line having been temporarily repaired. I looked in vain for a locomotive, or the remains of one, and did not know till I arrived at Kobe the following morning that it had gone clean out of sight in the sand. The injured were being cared for at Itozaki, where a surgeon-general and other doctors, together with a staff of nurses, from Hiroshima were in attendance. I read with much interest what a Japanese paper (*Osaka Asahi*) had to say two days later in a leader on the catastrophe. It pointed out that people who had discharged the duties of soldiers, and had fought bravely for their country, and had returned home in consequence of wounds or sickness, were entitled to the greatest honour. Such people were their country's treasure, rare treasure. It went on to say that many treasures were lost in the sea, many a soldier of honour was buried in the waters. It was a great misfortune to the State, and a great loss to the nation. One could scarcely bear to imagine the condition of their parents, brothers, wives, children, and friends, who had eagerly awaited their return from the scene of war, upon the news of the disaster reaching them. Surviving the dangers from weapons of war to which they were ready to sacrifice their lives, they had been lost by that accident. It was a matter of extreme sadness. Typhoons and storms are certain to come once or more in a year, and husbandmen prepare themselves for such calamities. Examples were not wanting of railways having sustained damage from typhoons. The locality where the accident took place that time was near the sea. In constructing a railway in such a district every precaution should have been taken. The line should have been specially strong and solid, so as to preclude as far as possible any such calamity. The journal was forced to conclude that the construction of the line was defective. If it was impossible to resist the wind and the waves, why was the coast line preferred to other routes? The approach of storms is indicated, and officers of the company ought to have been sent to make provision for possible danger. The writer of the article could not believe that the accident was due to natural causes, pure and simple, and contended that the Sanyô Railway Company should be held responsible for it. However, it had often been the habit of private railway concerns to forget that their enterprise was of a public nature, and they had subordinated questions of improvement to the immediate demand for profits and larger rates of dividend.

Other Japanese papers were equally unsparing in their criticism of the railway company, but it was by no means certain that the company was in any way responsible for the disaster. The Government Railway Inspector (Mr. Haraguchi), who was almost immediately upon the spot, was said to absolve the

Sanyô line of all blame, but the inquiry was proceeding when I left the country. This was the first railway accident of any importance that had taken place in Japan. Certainly, the country cannot boast a large mileage just yet, but the manner in which the Japanese have worked the half a dozen railway systems which they have got has earned the admiration of Europeans generally.

It was three o'clock the following morning before I had a train to take me on from Okayama to my destination. The long interval was spent in the waiting-room, in which were several other East-bound passengers. I tried to sleep, but in vain—the mosquitoes of Okayama are specially vicious and bloodthirsty. The stationmaster offered me a covering that would have been proof even against the proboscis of the *ka*, but as I could only use it at the risk of being smothered, I had no alternative but to remain exposed to the stings of my tormentors. It was a great relief when, as the day broke, I found myself ensconced in the corner of a comfortable railway carriage. In six hours I arrived, more asleep than awake, at Kobe, where the one absorbing topic of talk was the terrible accident. Friends who knew that I was somewhere on the road were relieved to find that I was not in it, as the fact that it was an exclusively military train was not then known. Again, I was the recipient of unbounded hospitality at the "Firs," Shinomiya. The pleasure of finding myself once more surrounded by Western comforts would have been complete but for the consciousness that in a native house a few yards off was a case of cholera.

Up to that date, however, the pestilence had not claimed a single European victim, and even among the natives its ravages had been almost confined to the poor and ill-fed. Among the more intelligent there was a general belief in the scientific treatment of the malady, but the mass of the people still put their faith in the charmed paper which they bought from the priests at the temples, or in the picture of Buddha which they swallowed.

CHAPTER XV.

THE RETURN.

Preparing to return—Nagoya—An unpleasant prospect—The Castle—An interesting vicissitude—Potteries—Strange spectacle—*Cloisonné*—Process described—Fuji-San—Leave-takings—A pleasing discovery—"*Sayônara*" to Nippon—The *Empress of Japan*—Prince Pak of Korea—Story of a royal refugee—Letter from the Prince—A Norman count—A Japanese surgeon—"How we took Port Arthur"—Beguiling the tedium of the voyage—Enveloped in smoke—False report—Hurrying home—Arrival.

My time in Japan was now drawing to a close. It had been my intention to take the *Empress of Japan*—in which I was to cross the Pacific—at Kobe, but I found that the time which would be allowed for landing at Yokohama would not be sufficient for certain business yet to be done there and at the capital, and so the long and tedious journey along the whole length of the Tôkaidô had again to be undertaken. I was able, however, to make a "stop-over" of one night at Nagoya, which I had passed through on my journey west. It was a seemingly interminable *kuruma* ride from the station to the house of the Rev. J. M. Baldwin, to whom I was the bearer of a letter of introduction, but who turned out to be from home on a holiday at Gotemba, at the foot of Fuji. I was faced by the unpleasant prospect of having to fall back upon a notorious, rat-infested, so-called European inn, which I had been advised to avoid, but as the coolie was turning away with me, it occurred to Mr. Baldwin's native caretaker to conduct us some distance away to a countryman of Mr. Baldwin—the Rev. H. J. Hamilton—both of whom were members of the Canadian Wyckliffe Mission. Mr. Hamilton received me most cordially. His house—half native, half American—was comfort itself.

Nagoya is one of the most flourishing cities of the Empire, being the largest on the Tôkaidô. The Castle (*Shiro*), which dates from the year 1610, and was erected by twenty powerful *daimyôs* as a residence for Ieyasu's son, is one of the wonders of the country. Though it has suffered much in the past at the hands of vandals, it is now carefully preserved by the Imperial authorities as a monument of historic interest. I had to be content with an exterior view only, as I was not provided with a permit, which can only be obtained at the prefecture, or Government office. Conspicuous by its glitter on the keep are two golden dolphins, dating from the erection of the castle, one of which has had an interesting vicissitude. It was sent to the Vienna Exhibition of 1873, and on its way back was wrecked in the *Messageries Maritimes* steamer *Nil*. It was recovered with much difficulty, and restored to its former position amid the rejoicings of the people.

Before quitting the city the following morning, I was taken to see some potteries, Nagoya being noted for its manufacture of porcelain. The obliging manager was at infinite pains to make every process as plain as it could be made to an untutored mind. The workroom was a strange sight—the men who moulded the clay were in almost complete undress, a narrow strip of loin-cloth being the only covering. A visit was also made to a *cloisonné* factory, which turns out work which is the admiration of the Western world. Here again a foreman explained to us the very complicated process of manufacture, but I fear that his explanation, lucid enough to my companion, who knew Japanese, was thrown away as far as I was concerned. Those of my readers who may wish to have some idea how that beautiful work is produced will be glad to have Mr. Henry

Norman's description, than which nothing could be clearer.

"First the plain copper vase or bowl or tray is taken between the knees of the workman, who snips off bits of brass the sixteenth of an inch wide from a long roll before him, bends them with tweezers and glues them on edge to the copper, thus making the outlines and detail lines of the finished sketch lying before him. An apprentice is putting the simple pattern in this way upon the flat bottom of a tray, while the most skilful workmen is poring over the delicate lines of the eyes and feathers of a cock on a plaque. This outline is next passed to a table between two workmen, who fill up the interstices with enamel, still following the coloured original before them from fifty little cups of coloured pigments. Then the work is fired, again painted with enamels, again fired, and so on, till little is seen but a daub-like distant copy. This is then polished down with the greatest care until the shining edge of the brass strips is reached, and at precisely the same point the colours are a perfect copy of the painting. *Cloisonné* making is labour of the most minute kind added to exquisite skill in the handling and combining of pigments. The result in its highest form is a painting more delicate than water-colours, and more lasting than brass. Formerly only geometrical and decorative designs were thus made; now birds and fish and snow scenes have been reached." *

Leaving Nagoya at 11.30 in the morning, I reached Yokohama a little before midnight. Fuji-San was invisible. Thick clouds covered its majestic cone from base to summit. Travellers, when quitting

---

* 'The Real Japan,' by Henry Norman.

the shores of Japan, gaze in the direction of Fuji for a final view of the "Peerless Mountain," with the same instinct and the same affection as they look towards the shore for a last fond glimpse of a beloved friend, but a vision of it is not always possible. The two days after my return to Yokohama were occupied mainly in leave-takings there and at the capital. I had not been many days on those hospitable shores before I had made troops of new friends, who took no little interest in my expeditions to distant parts of the Empire, and who expected me to report myself immediately on my return. On the eve of my coming away I discovered in cosmopolitan Yokohama the son of a dear old tutor of mine—Rev. Chancellor Lias of Llandaff—at whose rooms one of the most pleasant of my evenings in Japan was spent. On the morrow, after a final round of the curio shops in the Benten-dôri and the Honcho-dôri, I embarked on the *Empress of Japan* for Vancouver. Among the passengers who had preceded me on board was a young Korean prince, Yong Ho Pak by name, a refugee from his distracted country. His Christian friends in Yokohama had told me of him, and asked me to take a kindly interest in him, and to render him every assistance in my power. That, I need hardly say, I had great

Q

pleasure in doing. The dapper little man in European garb, with pronounced Korean features, who was addressed on board as "Your Highness," proved to be a well-known personality to those among the passengers who knew the Far East, having, though still young, played a great *rôle* in the government of his country. Unfortunately, his knowledge of English was very limited. A Victoria paper (*Daily Colonist*), in announcing our arrival at that port, gave the following account of him :—

"Prince Pak-Yong-Ho, Japan's firmest friend at the Korean Court, who was forced to fly from Seoul a short time ago, owing to the unexpected turn of the wheel in that much-disturbed city, reached Victoria by the *Empress of Japan*, and proceeds through to New York by to-day's express. What his plans are he cannot himself explain in detail—the business of the moment is to find a haven beyond the reach of the indignant Queen,* and such a shelter he believes America will afford. Troubles have come upon him in clouds during the past eventful year, and perfect rest, undisturbed by dreams of the assassin's dagger, has now an incomparable charm for the fallen minister. To but one of the many charges of his enemies does he enter a vigorous denial—he was not planning, nor had he ever contemplated, the centralization of the government of the Hermit Kingdom in himself, and so was not guilty of treason to his country and his Queen.

"It was during a ten years' enforced residence in Japan that

---

* Since assassinated.

Prince Pak of Korea became a lover of the Japanese, their progressive government and their modern institutions; and it was this fondness for all things Japanese that got him into trouble on his coming out of exile to assume the duties of Home Minister at his native capital. Everything ran smoothly for a time, and reforms having their origin in Japan were introduced in quick succession. Then it was whispered into the ear of the Queen that Pak was not disinterested—that, with Japan's aid, he might even raise his eyes to the throne—and the prince's fate was sealed.

"Then the report was freely circulated that Pak-Yong-Ho had been laying a trap for Russia in the interest of Japan, the Queen having only admiration for the land of the Czars and hatred and contempt for the New Japan. So Pak stock declined several points, and the Queen again securing the reins of government immediately decided upon a policy essentially pro-Russian and anti-Japanese, in which the Home Minister could have no part. For diplomacy's sake he made pretence of roundly abusing the Japanese, and made certain overtures of friendship to M. Waeber, the Russian Chargé d'Affaires. The latter was well prepared, however, and avoided what he and all others in Seoul took to be a Japanese trap.

"Concerning the subsequent crisis at Seoul, in which, though absent in person, Prince Pak played so prominent a part, the *Kobe Chronicle* of the 12th July has the following:—

"'In pointing out in our issue of the 8th inst. the serious position of affairs in Korea, and the possibility that a spark in that quarter might again set the Far East in a blaze, we little thought that events were then actually occurring at Seoul proving the accuracy of our reading of the signs. The Queen has thrown off the mask; the Ming party is for the time triumphant; and all officials in favour of Japan are in danger of arrest. On Saturday night a meeting of ministers was hurriedly convoked at the royal palace, all the ministers but Prince Pak and Jo Kohan being present. There it was determined that Prince Pak should be relieved of office, and his arrest was also ordered on a charge of treason. Prince Pak, however, appears to have got wind of the combination against him, and immediately fled from the capital to Chemulpo, which he reached on Sunday evening, taking refuge in a Japanese house there. It was expected that he would leave Chemulpo for Japan the same night. It is charged against Prince Pak by the Ming party that evidence has come to light showing that he was meditating a *coup d'état* with the object of seizing the reins of power, but as he was a minister, and already possessed almost supreme influence, the accusation is not likely to prove founded on truth.'"

Such was the interesting charge entrusted to me at Yokohama. He soon made himself at home on board, entered freely into the games, and though he associated chiefly with the Japanese merchants, whose language he seemed to know perfectly, he made a few friends among my own countrymen, notwithstanding his very broken English. He is young (about thirty-eight), and may yet be the chief force in Korean politics. Shortly after my return home I received from him a letter, dated from the Korean Legation at Washington, in the course of which he said:—

"I hope I may be in the near future able to visit Great Britain and the continental countries. If I should go, I will certainly inform you of my departure from New York beforehand. Recently another revolt has occurred in Korea, and it looks as though the Government has been changed since the last week or so. The reports are yet meagre, and I cannot form any definite opinion as to the future outlook for Korea. May God bless them and give them peace. I hope you will remember Korea and her poor suffering people in your prayers, and tell your Christian friends to take an interest in her. My hope and prayers are that some day Korea may worship the name of Jesus as her Lord and Saviour.

"I am trying hard to learn English, yet I am sorry to say that I have not made much progress so far. I am living in Washington at present."

Another "personage" among the passengers was Count Henry de la Vaulx, of Normandy, who was making the "grand tour," and whose *forte* was French colonisation. He had been going the round of the French colonies and protectorates of Cambodia, Cochin-China, and Tonkin. He was always ready to be drawn out on his favourite topic, and I had more than one discussion with him on the subject of the Frenchman *versus* the Englishman as a coloniser, but the Count knew no English and my French was not of the best. Like his countrymen generally, he felt sore on the subject of Egypt, and every argument in favour of the English view only met with a shrug of the shoulders.

Another interesting saloon passenger was a Japanese army surgeon, who was proceeding to qualify in London. He spoke English very well, told us all about the war, and "how we took Port Arthur."

Thus was the tedium of my second trans-Pacific voyage beguiled. Everything favoured a pleasant passage—a few interesting fellow-passengers (not *always* to be met with on an ocean voyage), a ship of unsurpassed comfort, and, above all, most propitious weather and an unruffled sea. The only circumstance that detracted from the entire enjoyment of the passage, was that, as we approached our destination, we found ourselves enveloped by the smoke of a burning forest, which is so apt to impede the navigation in the Gulf of Georgia, and which hangs about in that region for days after the fire has burnt itself out. Our arrival was delayed by it about twenty-four hours, and the rumour reached Vancouver that we had gone on the rocks. No risk, however, was run—the *Empress* too cautiously felt her way to come to grief, till a breeze suddenly arose and in a few moments cleared off the smoke, and Mount Baker in all his magnificence stood forth to our view. We were welcomed by practically the whole town of Vancouver, which takes a special pride in its great White Liners. There I took my leave of my precious royal charge, who was to proceed to Washington by way of San Francisco, and, transferring him to other hands, took the first train for Montreal, and the first boat thence home—thoroughly "done up," of course, but full of pleasant memories, never to pass away, of the journey, and especially of the far-distant, delightful, fascinating, and picturesque land through which I had wandered.

CHAPTER XVI.

THE RELIGIONS OF JAPAN.

Shintô—Buddhism—Christianity.

As the subject of the religions of Japan was one in which I was specially interested during my tour, and as it is one that I have been much questioned about since my return, I propose to treat briefly of each of them in this chapter, concluding with a few facts with regard to Christianity in that country.

There are two heathen religions in Japan, Shintô and Buddhism. Shintô is a Chinese word, meaning the "Way of the Gods," the Japanese term being *Kami no michi*. It is the indigenous creed of the country, and is a compound of nature-worship and ancestor-worship. It has countless deities (the Japanese say "eight millions," that is, an infinite number), the chief being *Ama-terasu*, the goddess of the sun, from whom is descended the Mikado. There are gods and goddesses of the wind, the ocean, fire, thunder and lightning, as well as of mountains, rivers, etc. New names are constantly being added to the pantheon, heroes and great men being deified without number.

The Shintô priests do not differ in appearance from laymen, but wear a long robe when presenting the daily sacrifices. Some temples have their priestesses, young girls whose duties consist in performing certain pantomimic dances. Neither they nor the priests are under vows. They marry and are given in marriage. There is no congregational worship, properly so called, but the services consist in the presentation of offerings of rice, fish, fruits, and so on, and in the recital of certain formulas which are a mixture of prayer and praise, but which are quite unintelligible to the people. Shintô demands little more of its devotees than a visit to the local temple on the occasion of its annual festival. It has no ethical or doctrinal code. It recognises life beyond the grave, but knows no hell or purgatory. It has no teachings concerning a future state. "Thou shalt honour the gods," "Thou shalt obey the Mikado," are practically the only commandments of Shintô.

To one who inquired of a Shintôist why his creed had no moral code, the reply was, "In China they truly did invent a moral system, for those wicked men needed it; in Japan we naturally follow the way of the gods."

Throughout the Middle Ages there was a form of Shintô known as Ryôbu Shintô, being the original creed corrupted by contact with Buddhism. For a thousand years most of the Shintô temples were served by Buddhist priests, and their architecture affected by Buddhist (or Indian) principles. The original pure and simple style gave way to an elaborate and ornate one. The pagoda, a Buddhist feature, became part of Shintô shrines. At the revolution of 1868, which restored the Mikado to his ancestral position as the real as well as the nominal ruler of the Empire, Shintô was purged of its Buddhistic accretions, and re-established as the national religion. Buddhist priests were ejected from the Shintô shrines, and pagodas, belfries, and such other features as did not belong to the original Shintô architecture were removed. Many of the temples were thus despoiled of much of their beauty.

The great characteristic of pure Shintô architecture is its simplicity. The temples consist of bare, unpainted, wooden rooms, covered with a thatch of chamæcyparis bark. There is no altar, idol, or ornament. The great symbol of the temple is the peculiar gateway called *torii*, which is placed at the entrance of the temple avenue. It is also known as "bird's rest," as the sacred birds were accustomed to perch on it. Some of the most important temples have several of these gateways. Their origin and signification are alike unknown.

For every one Shintô temple at Tôkyô there are nine Buddhist. Sir E. Satow, our minister at Tôkyô and the greatest authority on the subject, writes that "Buddhism, during the last ten years, has been steadily regaining power and position, while the Shintô religion, for the protection of which a government department, ranking with the Council of State, was thought necessary at the Revolution, has relapsed into its former insignificance. It is still in a certain sense a national religion, since its temples are maintained out of the imperial and local revenues, and the attendance of the principal officials is required by Court etiquette at certain annual festivals celebrated at the palace. But it has no exclusive hold over any section of the people, who adhere to it just in the same degree, and no more, as has been their practice during the last thousand years."

Buddhism was imported into Japan from India, by way of China and Korea, in the sixth century, A.D. It soon supplanted Shintô, and became the popular religion, being adopted even by the Mikados, lineal descendants of the Shintô goddess of the sun. In the ninth century it made rapid progress under the teaching of Kôbô Daishi, its greatest saint and apostle, who had spent some time in China studying its tenets. He is credited with the invention of the *Hiragana* syllabary, and has thus been the chief means of disseminating the Buddhist scriptures throughout Japan. He taught that the native Shintô deities were *avatars*, or incarnations, of Buddhist deities, and thus made it possible for those Shintôists who became converts to the imported religion to preserve to some extent their ancient faith.

Japanese Buddhism is split up into various sects and sub-sects, of which the chief are the *Tendai* and the *Shingon* (which are of Chinese origin), the *Jôdo*, *Nichiren*, and *Shin*. They hold widely different views upon the doctrine of Nirvana, some believing in the utter annihilation of the soul, others in its separate existence, but as part of the divine. But, according to Sir E. Satow, the points in dispute between them are highly metaphysical, the principles of one sect being considered incomprehensible except to such as have attained to Buddhahood.

The Shin sect has been called the Protestantism of Japan, because its priests are permitted to marry, and because its distinctive doctrine is that man is to be saved by faith in Amida, and not by works, or vain repetition of prayers. It is the most important sect in Japan, both from the number of its devotees, and its hold upon the ruling classes. Its founder, Shinran Shônin, has been honoured during the present reign by the bestowal of a posthumous title which means "the Great Teacher who sees the truth." The fine temples of the Shin sect are among the chief sights of the large cities of the Empire.

But though Japan is studded with temples, the Japanese are not a strongly religious people. Their attitude towards the supernatural has been described as a mixture of "fear and fun." Great numbers of them are indifferentists—so much so that the question has recently been discussed: Have the Japanese a religion? And the answer given by a missionary of the American Church in Japan is that "the Japanese come as near to being a nation of atheists as any people upon the planet." According to that authority (Rev. Henry Scott Jefferys), they have no god whatever in the Christian sense, or in the sense of the ancient European mythologies. Shintô is not really a religion, but a system of ceremonial observances centring in the Mikado. So far as can be made out, Shintôists do not pray for any definite thing at their shrines. They indulge in "vain repetitions," but a distinct petition there is none. Educated Japanese pride themselves upon their superiority to superstition, and recognise no god above the Mikado. But even he is not a god in the Christian sense, though he is known as Ten Shi Sama, or the Son of Heaven, and his palace is called Miya, or Temple. He, in his turn, has no object of worship except his ancestry. In that respect he differs from the Emperor of China, who worships Shang Ti, the Lord of Heaven.

The same may be said of Buddhism—the cult of the middle and lower class—as of Shintô—it has no god in the Christian sense. Buddha is not a God, and Buddhism is not a religion, as we understand it.

"Japanese exalt politeness and reverence above all things, and it seems but natural to a people in the habit of hitting their heads twice or thrice upon the straw mats every time a visitor of their own rank comes to call upon them, to continue to reverence their friends, relatives, parents, and rulers after their departure into the great unknown beyond; this looks to us like worship, but it is often nothing more than post-mortem politeness. Japanese near the Treaty Ports, out of consideration for their foreign friends, may concede the existence of the foreign god, but in the back country the ideas fade away, and they worship 'they know not what'; but they certainly do not worship in our religious sense, for they have no god." *

"The fact remains," writes Miss Bird, "that thirty-four

---

* *The Japan Evangelist*, April 1895.

millions of Japanese are sceptics or materialists, or absolutely sunk in childish and degrading superstitions, out of which the religious significance, such as it was, has been lost."

According to the same authority, there are 8,000 Shintô temples in Japan, attached to which there are about 20,000 priests and attendants. A few years ago there was granted annually for the support of those shrines a sum of £58,000. Formerly a Department of Public Worship dealt with such matters. They are now under the charge of the Home Secretary.

The priests are said to be, as a body, men of considerable culture and ability. Though I came in contact with many at the temples, I was never fortunate enough to meet with one who knew English. I have heard them highly spoken of as preachers, and certainly, if one may judge from translations of Japanese sermons given by Mitford, they have a quaint and telling way of putting things. In the list of Japanese proverbs given by Sir E. J. Reed in his elaborate work on Japan, occurs the following, " Clever preacher, short sermon." The following are extracts from a rather long sermon published by a priest of the Shingaku sect—which combines all that is good in Buddhism, Shintô, and Confucianism, and maintains the original goodness of the human heart, but, notwithstanding its length, it is not wanting in cleverness.

"Môshi* says, 'Benevolence is the heart of man; righteousness is the path of man. How lamentable a thing is it to leave the path and go astray, to cast away the heart and not know where to seek for it!'

"The text is taken from the first chapter of Kôshi (the commentator)† on Môshi.

"Now this quality, which we call benevolence, has been the subject of commentaries by many teachers; but as these commentaries have been difficult of comprehension, they are too hard to enter the ears of women and children. It is of this benevolence that, using examples and illustrations, I propose to treat.

"A long time ago there lived at Kyôto a great physician called Imaôji—I forget his other name: he was a very famous man. Once upon a time, a man from a place called Kuramaguchi advertised for sale a medicine which he had compounded against the cholera, and got Imaôji to write a puff for him. Imaôji, instead of calling the medicine in the puff a specific against the cholera, misspelt the word cholera so as to make it simpler. When the man who had employed him went and taxed him with this, and asked him why he had done so, he answered with a smile—

"'As Kuramaguchi is an approach to the capital from the country, the passers-by are but poor peasants and woodmen from the hills: if I had written "cholera" at length, they would have been puzzled by it; so I write it in a simple way, that should pass current with every one. Truth itself loses its value if people don't understand it. What does it signify how I

---

* The Chinese philosopher Mêng Tse, called by Europeans Mencius.

† Confucius

spelt the word cholera, so long as the efficacy of the medicine is unimpaired?'

"Now, was that not delightful? In the same way the doctrines of the sages are mere gibberish to women and children who cannot understand them. Now, my sermons are not written for the learned: I address myself to farmers and tradesmen, who, hard pressed by their daily business, have no time for study, with the wish to make known to them the teachings of the sages; and, carrying out the ideas of my teacher, I will make my meaning pretty plain, by bringing forward examples and quaint stories. Thus, by blending together the doctrines of the Shintô, Buddhist, and other schools, we shall arrive at something near the true principle of things. Now, positively, you must not laugh if I introduce a light story now and then. Levity is not my object: I only want to put things in a plain and easy manner.

"Well, then, the quality which we call benevolence is, in fact, a perfection; and it is this perfection which Môshi spoke of as the heart of man. With this perfect heart, men, by serving their parents, attain to filial piety; by serving their masters they attain to fidelity; and if they treat their wives, their brethren, and their friends in the same spirit, then the principles of the five relations of life will harmonise without difficulty. As for putting perfection into practice, parents have the special duties of parents; children have the special duties of children; husbands have the special duties of husbands; wives have the special duties of wives. It is when all these special duties are performed without a fault that true benevolence is reached; and that again is the true heart of man.

"For example, take this fan: any one who sees it knows it to be a fan; and, knowing it to be a fan, no one would think of using it to blow his nose in. The special use of a fan is for visits of ceremony; or else it is opened in order to raise a cooling breeze: it serves no other purpose. In the same way, this reading-desk will not do as a substitute for a shelf; again,

R

it will not do instead of a pillow: so you see that a reading-desk also has its special functions, for which you must use it. So, if you look at your parents in the light of your parents, and treat them with filial piety, that is the special duty of children; that is true benevolence; that is the heart of man. Now although you may think that, when I speak in this way, I am speaking of others, and not of yourselves, believe me that the heart of every one of you is by nature pure benevolence. I am just taking down your hearts as a shopman does goods from his shelves, and pointing out the good and bad qualities of each; but if you will not lay what I say to your own accounts, but persist in thinking that it is all anybody's business but yours, all my labour will be lost.

"Listen! You who answer your parents rudely, and cause them to weep; you who bring grief and trouble on your masters; you who cause your husbands to fly into passions; you who cause your wives to mourn; you who hate your younger brothers, and treat your elder brothers with contempt; you who sow sorrow broadcast over the world;—what are you doing but blowing your noses in fans, and using reading-desks as pillows? I don't mean to say that there are any such persons here; still there are plenty of them to be found—say in the back streets in India for instance. Be so good as to mind what I have said.

"Consider carefully, if a man is born with a naturally bad disposition, what a dreadful thing it is! Happily, you and I were born with perfect hearts, which we would not change for a thousand—no, not for ten thousand pieces of gold: is not this something to be thankful for? . . .

"When a man marries a wife, he thinks how happy he will be, and how pleasant it will be keeping house on his own account; but, before the bottom of the family kettle has been scorched black, he will be like a man learning to swim in a field, with his ideas all turned topsy-turvy, and, contrary to all his expectations, he will find the pleasures of housekeeping to be all a delusion. Look at that woman there. Haunted by her cares, she takes no heed of her hair, nor of her personal appearance. With her head all untidy, her apron tied round her as a girdle, with a baby twisted into the bosom of her dress, she carries some wretched bean sauce which she has been out to buy. What sort of creature is this? This all comes of not listening to the warnings of parents, and of not waiting for the proper time, but rushing suddenly into housekeeping. . . .

"There are plenty of people who use these words, *myself* and *my own*, thoughtlessly and at random. How false is this belief that they profess! If there were no system of government by superiors, but an anarchy, these people, who vaunt themselves and their own powers, would not stand for a day. In the old days, at the time of the war at Ichi-no-tani, Minamoto no Yoshitsuné left Mikusa, in the province of Tamba, and attacked Settsu. Overtaken by the night among the mountains, he knew not what road to follow; so he sent for his retainer, Benkei, of the temple called Musashi, and told him to light the big torches which they had agreed upon. Benkei received his orders and transmitted them to the troops, who immediately dispersed through all the valleys, and set fire to the houses of the inhabitants, so that one and all blazed up, and, thanks to the light of this fire, they reached Ichi-no-tani, as the story goes. If you think attentively, you will see the allusion. Those who boast about *my* warehouse, *my* farm, *my* daughter, *my* wife, hawking about this 'my' of theirs like pedlars, let there once come trouble and war in the world, and, for all their vain-gloriousness, they will be as helpless as turtles. Let them be thankful that peace is established throughout the world. The humane Government reaches to every frontier: the officials of every department keep watch night and day. When a man sleeps under his roof at night, how can he say that it is thanks to himself that he stretches his limbs in slumber? You go your rounds to see whether the shutters are closed and the front door fast, and, having taken every precaution, you lay yourself down to rest in peace, and what a precaution after all! A board, four-tenths of an inch thick, planed down front and rear until it is only two-tenths of an inch thick. A fine precaution, in very truth!—a precaution which may be blown down with a breath. Do you suppose such a thing as that would frighten a thief from breaking in? This is the state of the case. Here are men who, by the benevolence and virtue of their rulers, live in a delightful world, and yet, forgetting the mysterious providence that watches over them, keep on singing their own praises. Selfish egotists!

"'My property amounts to five thousand ounces of silver. I may sleep with my eyes turned up, and eat and take my pleasure, if I live for five hundred or for seven hundred years. I have five warehouses and twenty-five houses. I hold other people's bills for fifteen ounces of silver.' So he dances a fling for joy, and has no fear lest poverty should come upon him for fifty or a hundred years. Minds like frogs, with eyes in the middle of their backs! Foolhardy thoughts! A trusty castle of defence indeed! How little can it be depended upon! And when such men are sleeping quietly, how can they tell that they may not be turned into those big torches we were talking about just now, or that a great earthquake will not be upheaved? These are the chances of this fitful world."

That the pulpit is a power in Japan would scarcely be maintained, but the homily from which the above extracts have been taken is a fair specimen, I understand, of a Japanese sermon, and proves that the Japanese priest knows how to preach as well as to serve at the altar.

The Japanese have their sacred books, like the Chinese and the Hindoos, and many of them are very learned in them. They are called the *Kojiki* and the *Nihongi*. The former is the compilation of a woman, said to have been a peasant, and was published in 712 B.C. The *Nihongi* was mainly the work of one Toneri Shinnô, and was completed in A.D. 720. These sacred books contain, besides religious teaching and moral precepts, much of the early history of Japan. The *Kojiki* teaches that, before the world came into being there existed a God called "The Lord of the Centre of Heaven." After him two other deities appeared, "Lofty Producer" and "Divine Producer," who were joint creators of the earth and all that lived upon it.

Christianity was first introduced into Japan in the year 1549 by St. Francis Xavier. The story of his Mission is one of the most profoundly interesting passages in Japanese history. He was carrying on a propaganda in India when he met a Japanese fugitive named Anjiro, a native of Satsuma, who had learnt Portuguese and had become a Christian convert. Anjiro, in answer to Xavier's inquiry as to whether his countrymen would accept Christianity, declared (according to one of the missionary's letters) that "his people would not immediately assent to what might be said to them, but they would investigate what I might affirm respecting religion by multitudes of questions, and, above all, by observing whether my conduct agreed with my words. This done, the King, the nobility, and adult population, would flock to Christ, being a nation which always follows reason as a guide." Fired by the prospect, Xavier set out for the Land of the Rising Sun, and landed from a Chinese junk at Kagoshima, in the island of Kyûshû, with a few companions, including Anjiro as interpreter. After great privations—for it was the depth of winter—he arrived in about two months at the capital Miaco (Kyôto). By costly gifts he won the favour of the great warrior Nobunaga, who had brought a large part of the Empire under his sway, and was a bitter foe to Buddhism. After two years and a half of energetic proselytizing, Xavier returned to Portugal, together with a native ambassador, to make certain political arrangements in favour of the party who had lent him their support.

Other Jesuit missionaries went out in rapid succession, and their efforts were crowned with marvellous success. Not only the common people, but the *daimyôs*, high officers of the State, and of the army and navy, became converts. Christian churches studded the land, most of them being Buddhist temples which had been sprinkled and purified. Seminaries for the training of a native Christian priesthood were set up in the large towns. Towards the end of the Jesuit period, it is computed that the Christian converts numbered about six hundred thousand.

The death of Nobunaga was the turning-point in the history of the mission. His great generals, Hideyoshi and Ieyasu, were hostile to the new religion. In 1587 a great persecution broke out against the Christians, which lasted three years, and during which over twenty thousand were put to death. The Jesuits continued to send fresh missionaries into the country, in defiance of the rulers, who declared that, "should the very God of the Christians come, they would behead him." About that time was instituted the festival of the "Trampling of the Cross." I have already referred to the custom of trampling upon a cross, and other emblems of the Passion, by way of abjuring the proscribed religion. It is not many years since that festival was abolished. The last persecution of the Christians ended in the tragic incident of Shimabara, near Nagasaki. There, in the castle, the ruins of which still remain, the faithful had assembled from every quarter of the Empire for the purpose of a last and desperate stand against their persecutors. Being overpowered, they were all mercilessly massacred, multitudes of both sexes and all ages being hurled alive from the rock of Pappenberg into the sea. From that time, "the name of Christ became an object of shame and terror throughout Japan." According to that eminent authority, Dr. Griffis—

"For centuries the mention of that name would bate the breath, blanch the cheek with fear, as with an earthquake shock. It was the synonym of sorcery, sedition, and all that was hostile to the peace of society. All over the empire—in every city, town, village and hamlet, by the roadside, ferry, or mountain pass, at every entrance to the capital—stood the public notice-boards on which, with prohibition against the great crimes that disturb the relations of society and government, was one tablet, written with a deeper brand of guilt, with a more hideous memory of blood, with a more awful terror of torture, than when the like superscription was affixed at the top of a cross that stood between two thieves on a little hill outside Jerusalem. Its daily and familiar sight startled ever and anon the peasant to clasp hands and utter a fresh prayer, the *bonze* to add new venom to his maledictions, the magistrate to shake his head, and to the mother a ready word to hush the crying of her fretful babe. That name was Christ. So thoroughly was Christianity, or the 'Jashi mon' (corrupt sect), supposed to be eradicated before the end of the seventeenth century, that its existence was historical, remembered only as an awful scar on the national memory."

Such is the stirring story of the Jesuit Mission, which might never have come to such a tragical end, and might have resulted in the entire evangelization of the Japanese people, if its priests had not indulged in political intrigues, and invoked the aid of the secular power. From the massacre of Pappenberg rock, which all but extinguished the flame of Christianity in the land for well-nigh two centuries and a half, there was to be seen in every village, on every bridge, and on every sign-board, the terrible edict: "As long as the sun shall warm the earth, let no Christian be so bold as to come to Japan; and let all know that the King of Spain himself, or the Christian's God, or the great God of all, if he violate this command, shall pay for it with his head." *

It was in 1859 that the Gospel was again brought to the Japanese. The first missionaries were Ameri-

---

* In his 'Japan Missions' Mr. Eugene Stock has the following comment upon the above proclamation:—

"Who is 'the Christian's God,' so curiously distinguished in these shocking words from the 'great God of all'? One of the letters carried to Pope Gregory XIII. by the four Japanese nobles was thus addressed: 'A celui qui doit être adoré, et qui tient la place du Roi du Ciel, le grand et Très-Saint Pape'; and another began thus: 'J'adore le Très-Saint Pape, qui tient la place de Dieu sur la terre.'

"We can honour the zeal and self-denial of the Jesuit missionaries. We can believe that among their converts there were some who, in much ignorance, did trust their souls to the Saviour. But the responsibility for the blasphemous proclamation, which for two centuries and more shut out Christianity from Japan, must lie at the door of Rome."

cans, but they were only able to work in an indirect way. They had to use great tact and precaution. Though the blasphemous proclamation which was once so universal was no longer seen, on the Nihonbashi—the principal bridge of Yedo—there stood a notice-board, for some years after Lord Elgin's treaty had secured toleration for foreigners, strictly prohibiting "the evil sect called Christian." Gradually the authorities interfered less and less with the new religion; its propagation by the missionaries, and its profession by the people, came, after a while, to be tacitly tolerated, till, at length, under the new constitution of 1889, the fullest freedom of belief was accorded to subjects of the Japanese empire.

The body of Christians now in the country is 100,000 strong, or an average of one in 400. It is composed broadly of 60,000 Roman Catholics and Greek Christians, and 40,000 of all the other Christian denominations. The country is now covered with a network of mission stations, with the Open Ports as headquarters. There has been a consolidation of the missions of the Church of England and of the Protestant Episcopal Church of America under the title of "Nippon Sei Kôkwai" (the Church in Japan). There is also the "Nippon Ichi Kyôkwai,"

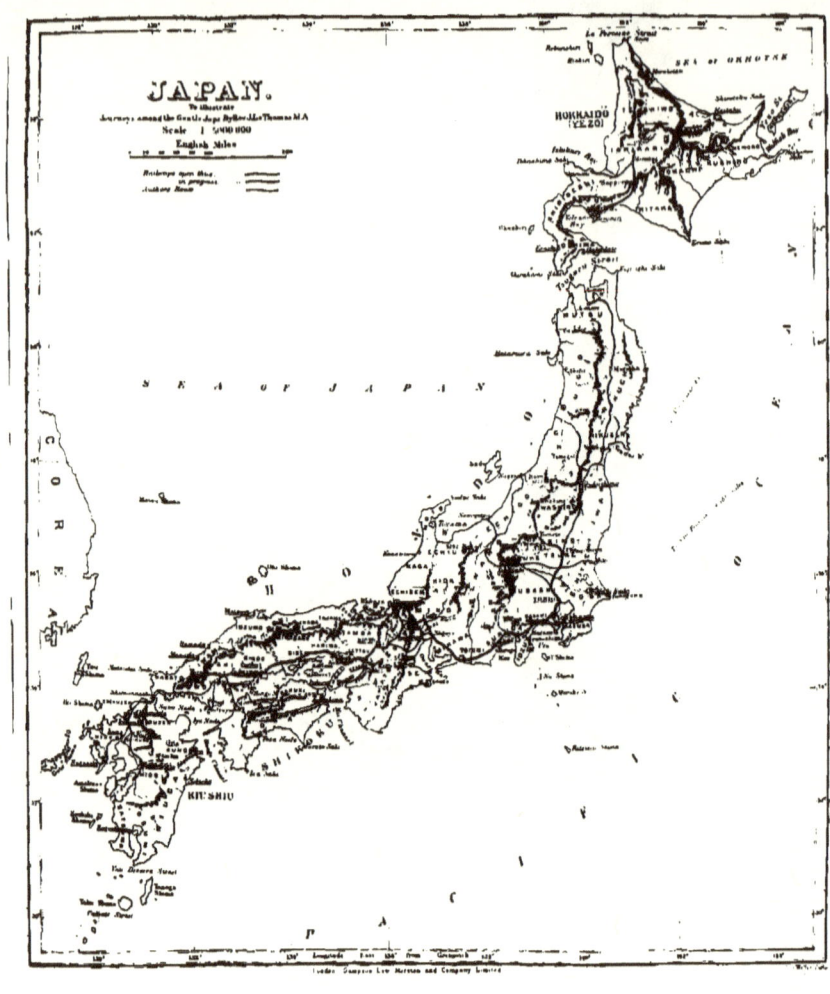

consisting of the American and Scotch Presbyterian Churches and the Dutch Reformed. Nearly every form of American Nonconformity is represented, and there has recently been an invasion by the Salvation Army.

INDEX.

Accident, railway, 215–219
Adams, Will, 44, 45
Ajina, 185, 186
Akashi, 169, 170
Aleutian Islands, 20, 22
Ama-terasu, Goddess of the Sun, 26, 232, 236
American Independence Day, 135
Americans, their interest in Japan, 2; resident in Japan, 28, 35, 156, 163
Amida, images of, at Nikkô, 122, 164, 237
"Amusements Committees," 23
Anglican Church at Yokohama, 35, 36
Anjiro, 245, 246
Annai-jô, 128, 209
Appeal to Japanese women, 94, 95
Arab, antithesis of Jap, 30
Architecture in Japan, 98; military, 201; Buddhist and Shintô, 234
Archives, 49, 187
Arima, 155, 164, 167, 185, 201
"Armada," Mongolian, 48
Arnold, Sir Edwin, 24, 45, 46, 48, 169, 190, 191
Art, Japanese, 187
Artists, 18
Artistes, 35, 206
Asakusa, 87–89
Asano Takumi, 104, 105
Ashinoyu, 73–76
Athletic sports on the Pacific, 22
Atlantic, the North, 3, 9, 14, 16, 17
"Atlantic Ferry," 13
Atoshi, 34
Atsumori, story of, 170
Attention, Japanese, 67
Attu, Island of, 20
Austin, Rev. W. T., at Yokohama, 36

INDEX

Avatars, 236
Avenue of Nikkô, 118
Awa, province of Shikoku, 192
Azabu, 91, 94

BACON, Miss, 75, 90
Baker, Mount, 230
Baldwin, Rev. J. M., 222
Ballard House, Kobe, 140, 170, 171
Banff, 5, 6
Bank, Imperial, 147
Banner, Japanese national, 194
Baring-Gould, Miss Edith M. E., extract from her 'Ever Westward through Heathen Lands,' 22
Baths and bathing, 70, 71, 155, 157, 161, 209
Battlefield, crossing a, 127
Bayeaux Tapestry, Japanese, 48
Bazaar of Tôkyô, 83
Beaver, steamship, 19
Bed, Japanese, 68, 131, 158
Behring Sea, 20
Bells, at Kyôto, 151; at Nara, 165
Benten, 55
Benten-dôri, Yokohama, 225
Benten-yama, 74
Bickersteth, Bishop Edward, 91–93
——————, Miss, her book on Japan, 166

Bill, 177, 178
Bird-life in Japan, 127, 128
Birushana; *see* "Roshana."
Bishop, Mrs., *née* Miss Bird, 93, 94, 238
Bismarck, 5
"Bismarck Hill," 161
Biwa Lake, 140
Bizarreries, 99, 100
Bluff, the, Yokohama, 34
Bon Matsuri (Festival of the Dead), 168, 169
Booking on Japanese railways, 213–215
Books, The Sacred, of Japan, 245
Boscawen, Mr. A. G., M.P., 148, 195, 196
Botanical Gardens, 102
"Boys" on the *Empress of India*, 15
Brandon, 7
Bret Harte, his 'Heathen Chinee,' 24
Bridges at Tôkyô, 82; Red Bridge at Nikkô, 120
"Britain of the Pacific," 2
British Columbia, 6, 9
—————— consulate, 61; embassy, 116
Brittan's, Miss, at Yokohama, 34
Brooklyn Bridge, 2
Bryan, Rev. Mr., 185
Buddha, colossal statue of, at

254   INDEX

Kamakura, 49, 50; at Nara, 163, 164, 238
Buddhism, central idea of, 50, 232, 235–239
Bûyo, 69

CABBY, rapacity of the, 33
Calgary, 7, 8
Calligraphy of Kôbô Daishi, 123, 124
Canada, 7
Canadian Pacific Railway, 2–5, 7, 10–12, 14
Canadians, 3
Cañon, Fraser River, 6
Cape Su-zaki, 27
Cards, visiting, 46, 104
Cascades, at Nikkô, 122, 126; at Chûzenji, 127; at Kobe, 143, 144
Castles, Odawara, 65; Osaka, 145, 146; Kyôtô, 151; Himeji, 173; Okayama, 179, 180; Matsuyama, 200, 201; Nagoya, 222, 223; Shimabara, 247
"Celestials," 15, 23, 24
Cemeteries, 103, 168
Chadai, tea-money, 128, 178
Chamberlain, Professor Basil Hall, 50, 102
Cherry-blossoms, 83
"Chicago of Japan," 144
China, 5, 23; works on, 26; interior of, 94; cholera brought to Japan from, 143; Mr. Fripp's travels in, 171; Emperor of, 238
Chinese, 4, 5; "boys," 15; death of a Chinaman, 23, 25; Chinese at Yokohama, 35; their commercial morality, 179
Chinese Seas, typhoons in the, 18
Chion-In, temple of, at Kyôtô, 151
Cholera, at Kobe, 143, 220; at Hiroshima, 184, 199, 215
Christianity, 27, 245–251
Christian relics, 84–86
Churches, at Tôkyô, 92; at Kobe, 141, 142
Chûzenji, 122, 125–127, 132–134
Cleanliness, 71
Cleveland, Mrs., 94
Climate, 71; of Shikoku, 208
Cloisonné, 223, 224
Clubs, at Yokohama, 35; at Kobe, 141
Coaster, Japanese, 196, 197, 210
College, Imperial Naval, 212
Colonisation, French, 229
Commandments of Shintô, 233
Commendatory letter, 123
Confirmation Service at Tôkyô, 92
Confucius, 108, 240

INDEX

Congregationalists, at Yokohama, 36; at Kobe, 141; at Nara, 163.
Constitution, promulgation of the, 135
Consulate, British, 61
Coolies, at Yokohama, 30; powers of endurance of, 31; titled, 31, 34, 65, 73, 76, 77; stupidity of, 149, 150, 156, 185, 189, 201
Court, Imperial, 97
Cranes, 180
Cree Indians, 7
Cricket, on the Pacific, 22; at Kobe, 141
Curios, Indian, 8; Japanese and Chinese, 81, 141
Currency, Japanese, 36, 37
Custom House examination, 29

DAI-BUTSU, at Kamakura, 49; at Nara, 163, 164
Daily Colonist (Victoria, B.C.), extract from the, 226-228
Daiya-gawa, the, 120, 122-124
Dances on the Pacific, 23
Date Masamune, Prince of Sendai, 85
Deer, at Nara, 164; in Miyajima, 187
Diet, Japanese, 54
Dilatoriness of the Japs, 194, 195

Divine Service, on the Pacific, 25; at Nikkô, 119; at Kobe, 141, 142, 143
Divinity School, Tôkyô, 93
Dôgo (Iyo), 209
Dollar, Mexican silver, 36
Donkey-boys of Egypt, 149
Dooman, Rev. Isaac, 162
Dragon's Head Cascade, 127
Drama, 103, 170
Dress, national *versus* foreign, 94-98
Dutch traders, 86

EARTHQUAKES, 58-61, 80, 92, 140, 166, 167
Ebisu, God of Luck, 162
Ebisu-ya, Enoshima, 53
Edict prohibiting Christianity, 249
Education, of Japanese ladies, 75; of *geishas*, 206
Electricity, at Vancouver, 11; in Japan, 68, 69, 80
Emma-Ô, 144, 169
Emperor of China, 238
Empress steamships, 14, 15, 18; library of, 26
Empress of India, 15; in a typhoon, 18; Divine Service on board the, 25
Empress of Japan, the, 90, 95, 99
Empress of Japan, 221, 225
Engineers, English, 37, 78

256 INDEX

English, difficulties of, 16; on Japanese railways, 44; study of, in Japan, 75, 76
English Bay, the, Vancouver, 12
Englishmen, land-hunters, 3, 16; in Yokohama, 35; at Ashinoyu, 74
Enoshima, 42, 52-55, 74
Epidemics, 80
Etajima, Island of, 212
Exeter, Bishop of, 166
Exhibition, at Kyôto, 139, 152, 153; at Tôkyô, 83, 153

Fans, 128, 141, 142
Far East, 5, 17, 20; landing in, 29, 35, 36, 47, 158, 184, 213, 226
Far West, 20, 47, 54, 67
Fares, *jinrickisha*, 32, 33; railway, 39
Festivals, 107, 168, 169; "Trampling of the Cross," 247
Feudal system, 31, 47, 108, 201
Fire, imaginary outbreak of, 25
Fire-box; see "Hibachi."
Fish in Lake Chûzenji, 127
Foreign Office at Tôkyô, 41, 116
Foreigners, difficulties of English to, 16

Forest, 11
Football on the Pacific, 22
Formosa, 182
Forty-seven Rônins, story of the, 103-109
Fraser River, 6
French at Yokohama, 35; language on Japanese railways, 44; ladies contrasted with Japanese, 99
Fripp, Mr. C. E., 171
Fudô, 144
Fuji, 65, 140, 222, 224, 225
Fujisawa, 55-57; demonstration at, 62
Fuji-ya, Miyanoshita, 73

Games, on the Pacific, 22, 23; at Kobe, 141; at Arima, 158
Gardens, Zoological, at Tôkyô, 86; Botanic, 112
Gardner, Rev. C. Graham, 142
Geisha, 203, 204-207
General Grant, his opinion of Li Hung Chang, 5; at Nikkô, 120
Germans, at Yokohama, 35; at Ashinoyu, 74; German at the Imperial University, Tôkyô, 100
Gin-kakuji, Silver Tower, at Kyôto, 151
Ginza, at Tôkyô, 81

INDEX

"Girl of the Period," Japanese, 96
"Glasgow of Japan," 144
Go-aheadedness, American, 6
Gods and goddesses: Hachiman, God of War, 49, 50; Ama-terasu, Goddess of the Sun, 26, 232, 236; Kwannon, Goddess of Mercy, 49, 87; Seven Gods of Luck, 144; Emma-Ô, 144, 169; Fudô, 144; Shusha Daio, 120
Golf, 23
Gotemba, 140, 222
Grafting, 181
Graphic, special artist of the, 171
"Great Divide," 9
Greeting, Japanese, 53, 66, 69, 77, 162, 202
Griffis, Dr., 248
Guinness, Mr., 125, 127
Gulf of Tôkyô, 27; of Georgia, 230
Gunboats, American, 2

HACHI-ISHI, 117
Hachiman, temple of, at Kamakura, 49, 50, 52
Hackman, rapacity of American, 33
Hades, Buddhist, 169
Hakarankwai, 150
Hakone Hills, 58–76

Hakodate, 40
Hamilton, Rev. H. J., 222
Hammam, mysterious inscription at Nikkô, 123
Handbooks, Miss Scidmore's, 205, 206; to Nikkô, 126; see "*Murray*."
Hara-kiri, 104, 106, 107, 115, 183, 184
Hartford, 4
Hashikura Rokuemon, 85
Hatago, 178
Hearn Lafcadio, 97
"Heathen Chinee," 24
Hibachi, 66, 67, 175–177
Hidetada, mausoleum of, 82
Hideyoshi, 26, 65, 145, 155, 173, 247
Himeji, 173
Hiragana, 51, 93, 236
Hiroshima, 172, 181, 182–189, 199, 213, 214
Hitomaro, 170
Hokkaidô (Yeso), 192
Holidays, national, 135
Holy Land, lecture on the, 93
Home Secretary at Tôkyô, 154, 239
Honcho-dôri, Yokohama, 225
Hondo, 201
Hongwangis, temples, at Kyôto, 151
Hospital at Tôkyô, 102
Hôtel Métropole, Tôkyô, 80

s

Hudson's Bay fort, 6; Company, 19
Hyôgo, 140

ICEBERG, 18
Iemitsu, 26, 82, 121
Ieyasu, 26, 82, 121, 122, 222, 247
Illuminations at Yokohama, 134
Indians, Cree, 7
Indifferentism, 237
Inland Sea, 169, 173, 192, 197, 201; Canon Tristram's opinion of, 211, 212
Inns, Japanese, 63, 65, 127, 128–131
Interpreters, 54, 55, 129
Ironclad, Japanese, 212
Italian on Japanese railways, 44
Ito, Marquis, 182, 194
Itozaki, 217
Iyo, province of Shikoku, 192, 200

JAPAN, works on, 26
"Japan Missions," 249 (note)
Japan Stream, 23, 193
'Japanese Girls and Women,' Miss Scidmore's, 75, 90
Japanese language, 37, 44, 72 75, 92, 129, 149, 159
'Japonaiseries d'Automne' of Pierre Loti, 118

Japs, on the "C. P. R.," 4; as railway travellers, 38; as chartographers, 52; contrasted with Europeans, 56; as fellow-travellers, 63, 64; as bathers, 71; their physique, 74; their women as linguists, 75; as religionists, 144, 237, 239; as horticulturists, 181; as sailors, 193
Jefferys, Rev. Henry Scott, 237
Jigen Daishi, 124
Jikuku Daishi, 110
Jingo Kôgô, first Empress of Japan, 26
Jinrickisha, 30
Johnson, Mr. Cameron, 142
Joss, 24
Junks, 28, 148, 199, 201

KAGO, 73, 74, 125, 156
Kagoshima, 246
Kagura, an ancient dance, 164
Kake-mono, 158
Kamakura, 42, 43, 46–52, 163, 164
Kanagawa, 78
Kanaya, the, at Nikkô, 118, 119, 128, 132, 133
Kauranjô, 104
Kasuga temple at Nara, 164
Katase, 52–54
Kawasaki, 78

INDEX 259

Kenchô, 61
Kicking-Horse Pass, 9
Kihara, 217
King, Rev. Armine F., 91
Kin-kakuji, Gold Tower, at Kyôto, 151
Kinka-zan, 27
Kirifuri-no-taki, Cascade, at Nikkô, 122
Kishu, 57
Kiyomizu-dera, at Kyôto, 152
Kobe, 137, 140–171; "Union Church," 141–143; Shinomiya, 142; Nunobiki, 143, 167, 169, 172, 173, 219, 220
Kobe Chronicle, 227
Kôbô Daishi, 26; temple dedicated to, 78; calligraphy of, 123, 124, 189, 236
Kodsu, 62, 64, 75–77
Kajiki, 245
Kompira, 209
Ko-Murasake, story of, 109–115
Koshigoe, 52, 55
Koraku-En Gardens, 180, 181
Korea, 208, 225–229, 235
Kôtsuké no Suké, 104–108
Kublai Khan, 48
Kumagai Naozane, 170
Kure, 212
Kuruma; see "*Jinrickisha.*"
Kwammu, Emperor, 150
Kwankôba, at Tôkyô, 83

Kwannon, 49; temple and image of, 52, 152
Kyôto, 79, 139, 140, 148; arrival in, 149; story of, 150; area, population, and historic buildings, 151; Industrial Exhibition, 152, 153; Yaami's, 153, 170, 246
Kyûshû, 192, 246; Railway, 182

LACQUER, 82
Land-hunters, English and Scandinavian, 3
Lakes, Chûzenji, 125–127, 133, 134; Yumoto, 127, 133; Biwa, 140; at Nara, 165
Languages, foreign, in Japanese schools, 75
Leave-taking in Japan, 55, 56, 76, 132, 178, 190, 206, 210
Lecture on the Holy Land, 93
Leprosy, 57, 92
Li Hung Chang, 4, 5, 182
Lochs Katrine and Vennachar of Japan, 133
Lotus, 87, 89
Luggage on Japanese Railways, 39, 77, 137, 138

MAGELLAN, 17
Makkura-daki Cascade at Nikkô, 122

260　INDEX

Manchuria, Mrs. Bishop's journey through, 94
Mats (*tatamis*), 54, 158, 160
Matsuyama, 200–208
Mausoleums of Ieyasu and Iemitsu, 117, 121, 122
Max O'Rell, 16
McClatchie's translations of Japanese plays, 95, 96
Meadows, Mr., at Osaka, 165
Medicine Hat, 9
Megane-bashi, at Tôkyô, 82
Meguro, 109–115
Mencius (Môshi), 240
Menjô, 40
Menu, on the *Empress* steamships, 16
Merchants, Japanese, 4
Meridian, crossing the, 21, 22
Methodists at Yokohama, 36
Métropole, Hôtel, Tôkyô, 80, 91
Middies, English, at Nikkô, 122
Mihara, 181, 182
Mikado, ancestress of the, 26, 232; 48; Court trappings of the, 86; palace of the, 89, 90, 120, 127, 135, 150, 165; at Hiroshima, 183, 194, 238
Minamoto clan, 170
Mineral springs, 71, 74, 127, 131, 155, 161
Mint, Imperial, 147

Misconceptions with regard to Japan, 97, 98
Mission-room, Seamen's, at Yokohama, 36
Mission, St. Andrew's, 91–93
Missionaries, Canadian, 7, 27, 66; Roman Catholic, 84, 85, 245–247, 250, 251; 140, 162, 163, 167, 185, 201, 202, 237
Mitford's 'Tales of Old Japan,' 104, 239
Mitsu-ga-hama, 199, 200, 210
Miyajima, 185–189
Miyanoshita, 65, 70, 71, 73
Miyoshino, at Okayama, 175–178
Moji, 182
Mongol, the, and English, 16
Mongolian features, 4; "Armada," 48
Montreal, 2–4, 6, 231
Moose Jaw, 9
Morality, of the *geisha*, 206; commercial, 179
Mosquitoes, 69, 167, 177, 209, 219
Moto-machi, street at Kobe, 141
Mount Baker, 19
Mount Royal, 2
Mounted Police, North-West, 7
Mousmés, 53, 64, 77, 129, 130, 144, 160, 202

INDEX 261

Mukogawa, Valley of the, 160, 161
Murray's Handbook, 72, 80, 88, 123, 143, 144, 175
Museum, of Uyeno, 84–86; of Okayama, 180
Mythology, Japanese, 55

NAGASAKI, 40, 173
Nagoya, 137, 138, 221–224
Naka-dôri, at Tôkyô, 81
Namma-ya, the, at Yumoto, 128
Nantai-zan, 126
Nara, 162–165
Nara-ya, Miyanoshita, 73
Narrows, The, Vancouver, 89
National Review, the, extract from, 148
Naval Reserve, officers of the, 15
—— station, Japanese, 212
Nestorian Christians, 163
New England, 4
—— World, 6, 10, 20
—— York, Japanese merchants in, 4
Newspapers, Japanese, 214, 217, 218
Niagara, 2
Nichi Nichi Shimbun ("Daily News"), 214
"Nightingale of Japan," 128
Nigwatsu-do, temple of, 165
Nihon-bashi, Tôkyô, 82, 250

Nihongi, 245
Niigata, 40
Nijo Castle, Kyôto, 151
Nikkô, 82, 116, 117; avenue, 118; the Kanaya, 118, 119; the Sacred Bridge, 120; mausoleums of Ieyasu and Iemitsu, 121, 122; cascades, 122; images of Buddha, 122; legend of Kôbô Daishi, 123, 124
"Nippon Sei Kôkwai," 250
"Nippon Ishi Kyôkwai," 250
Nirvâna, 138; doctrine of, 236
Nishinomiya, 161, 162
Nobunaga, 246, 247
Norman, Mr. Henry, 95, 224
North - West, 4; Mounted Police, 7
Nunobiki, Kobe, 143, 144

OBSERVATORY at Tôkyô, 102
Odawara, 65
Officers, army, 62, 203
Official fiction, 61
Officials, customs, 29; railway 39, 40; dress of, 97; 146
Ofuna, 46
Oguri Hangwan, 56, 57
Oigawa River, 139
Oishi Kuranosuké, 104–107
Okayama, 173, 175–181, 215, 219
Old Japan, 33, 87, 98
Omori, 78

Ondo, 212
Onomichi, 181, 182, 215, 216
Opium, smuggling of, 29
Oriental Hotel, Yokohama, 34; Kobe, 141
—————— life in Vancouver, 11
Orientals, 69, 148
Osaka, 40, 140, 144; area and population, 145; castle, 145, 146, 173; Imperial Mint, 147; bazaar, 148; residence of Archdeacon Warren, 165–167; 185
Osaka Asahi, 217
Otagawa, River, 184
Owari, province of, 140

PACIFIC, the, 4, 9, 10, 13, 14, 16–19, 22
Pagodas, 28, 165, 234
Pak, Yong Ho, Prince of Korea, 225–229
Palace, Imperial, at Tôkyô, 89, 90; at Kyôto, 151
Paper and printing works at Tôkyô, 147
Papooses, 7
Pappenberg, Rock of, 248, 249
Park, Vancouver, 11; Shiba and Uyeno, Tôkyô, 82, 83
Parthia steamship, 20
Passport, 40, 41, 42, 61, 116, 199
Perry, Commodore, 75
Philippine Islands, 17, 59

"Pidgin" English, 15, 24
Pierre Loti, 118
Pilgrimages, 107, 111, 126, 162
Pipe, 176, 177
Police, North-West Mounted, 7
Politeness of the Japanese, 29, 53, 63, 89, 124, 129, 130, 146, 178, 199
Pope, Japanese embassy to the, 85
Port Arthur, 195, 230
Portage-la-Prairie, 7
Potteries, 223
Prairies, 7, 8
Preaching, on the Pacific, 25; at Nikkô, 119; at Kobe, 143
Priests, 233, 239, 244
Priestesses, Shintô, 164, 165, 233
Promulgation of the Constitution, 135
Proverbs, Japanese, 124, 239
Pullman passengers, 4
Punctuality, Japanese want of, 193, 194
Punkahs, 141–143

"QUEEN City of the West," 20
Queen's English, 33, 89

RAILWAYS, Canadian Pacific, 2; Japanese, 37, 38, 78, 79, 116, 117, 137, 169, 182, 195, 196, 200

INDEX

Reading-room at Yokohama, 36
Red Bridge of Nikkô, 120
Reed, Sir E. J., 239
Relics, Christian, 84–86; of the Forty-seven Rônins, 104, 107, 108
Religious exercises, 110; ascent of Nantai-zan, 126
Revolution of 1868, 47, 50, 65, 150, 234
Rin; see "Currency."
Rivers of Japan, 120, 139; Yodogawa, 148; 161, 168; Otagawa, 184
Roads of Japan, 71, 125, 133, 160, 185
Rockies, scenery in the, 6; distance from Winnipeg, 7; crossing the, 8, 9
Rokko-san Pass, 156
"Rome of the Far East," 151
Roshana, image of, at Nara, 164
Russian cathedral, 116
Ryôbu Shintô, 49, 234
Ryôri-ya (restaurant), 202

SAKÉ, 203
Salvation Army, 251
Samisen, 205
Sampan, 28, 134, 148; Will Adams' description of, 186, 187; 201, 210, 212
Samurai, among the coolies, 31, 105, 107, 111, 114, 183, 184, 189
Sanjiusangendo, temple of, Kyôto, 151
San-kei, "three chief sights" of Japan, 187
Sannomiya, 140
Sanuki, province of Shikoku, 192
Sanyô railway, 169, 172, 173, 181, 182, 218, 219
Saris, Captain, description of Osaka castle, 146
Satow, Sir E., 235
Scandinavian land-hunters, 3
Scenery, along the "C. P. R.," 6; at Miyanoshita, 73; near Ashinoyu, 74; at Nikkô, 118, 126; at Arima, 157; along the valley of the Mukogawa, 160; in the Inland Sea, 169, 173
Schools, 75, 97, 161; school-children, 62, 63, 138, 161, 162, 186
Scidmore, Miss, her 'Westward to the Far East,' 17, 205, 206
Seamen's Mission, at Yokohama, 36; at Kobe, 142
'Seas and Lands,' Sir Edwin Arnold's, 191
Sects, Buddhist, 236, 237
Seismic wave, 167 (note)

Seismological Society, 60
Seiyô-ken, Tôkyô, 80, 87
Selkirks, the, 6, 9
Sen; see " Currency."
Sengakuji, 103–109
Senjô-ga-hara, Moor of the Battlefield, 127
Senkoji, temple of, 181
Sen-yugi, burial-place of the Mikados, 151
Sermon, Japanese, 240–244
Seven Gods of Luck, 144
Shanghai, contrasted with Kobe, 154
Sheep at the Zoological Gardens, Tôkyô, 86
Shiba Park, 82; temples photographed by Mrs. Bishop, 94; 169
Shikoku, island of, meaning of the name, 192; climate, 193; passage to, 196–198; port of Mitsu-ga-hama, 199; Matsuyama, 200–208; Dôgo, 209
Shimabara, castle of, 247
Shimbashi, 79, 81
Shimonoseki, 172, 182
Shinagawa, 78
Shinomiya, 142, 220
Shinran Shônin, 237
Shintô, 49, 50, 232–235, 237–239
Shirai Gompachi, story of, 109–115

Shizuoka, 137
Shôdô Shônin, legend of, 120
Shôguns, 26, 47; mortuary temples of, 82, 87; court trappings of, 86; castle of, 89; 127
Shovel-board on the Pacific, 22
Shusha Daio, 120
Shutters, 68–70, 112, 177, 207
Singing, 186
Smoking, 63, 64, 176
Snowsheds, 9
Somen-ga-taki, cascade, at Nikkô, 122
South Sea Islands, 12
Springs, mineral, 71; Ashinoyu, 74; Yumoto, 127, 131; Arima, 155, 157; Dôgo (Iyo), 209
Squaws, 7
St. Andrew's Mission, 91–93
Straits of Georgia, 19
Straw sandals, 124
Students, Japanese, 4, 46, 100, 101, 137, 138
Sugimoto-ya at Arima, 157
Suicide at the call of honour; see " Hara-kiri."
Suma, 169, 170
Sumiyoshi, 156
Sunday on the Pacific, 24, 25
Superstition at Nikkô, 123
Su-zaki, Cape, 27
Swallows' nests, 160
Swann, Rev. Sidney, 141

TAIRA clan, 170
Takarazuka, 160
'Tales of Japan,' Mitford's, 104
Tea on Japanese railways, 39; "tea-money," 128, 178
Tea-houses, 51, 56, 64, 72, 77, 111, 125, 143, 187, 202, 214
Telephone exchange, 80
Temples, of Hachiman, 49; of Kwannon, 52; at Shiba and Uyeno, 82, 87; of Kwannon at Asakusa, 87–89; Sengakuji, 106; at Nikkô, 121, 122; at Kyôto, 151, 152; at Nishinomiya, 162; at Nara, 164, 165; at Akashi, 170; at Onomichi, 181; in Miyajima, 187, 188
Terute Hime, 56, 57
Throne of the Mikado, 86
Time-table on the "C. P. R.," 10
Tobacco-mono, 176
Tôkaidô Railway, 43, 46, 55, 62, 77, 133–140, 151, 161, 173
Tôkyô, arrival at, 79; story of, 79; area and population, 79; foreign concession, 80; hotels, 80; Ginza and Naka-dôri, 81; bridges, 82; parks, 82–87; bazaar, 83; museum, 84–86; Zoological Gardens, 86; Imperial Palace, 89, 90; Bishop Edward Bickersteth's mission, 91–93; Imperial University, 100–102; Forty-seven Rônins, 103–109

Tôkyô, Gulf of, 27, 74
Tokugawa dynasty, 82, 201
Tonneri Shinnô, 245
Tonosawa, 65–71, 76
Tonquin, Gulf of, course of typhoon, 17
Torii, "bird's rest," 187, 188, 234, 235
Tosa, province of Shikoku, 192
"Trampling boards," 85, 247
"Treaty Ports," 40, 98, 140
Tristram, Canon, 181
Tsukiji, district of Tôkyô, 79, 80
Tsurumi, 78
Tunnels, 139, 174, 175, 182
Turkey, passport regulations in, 40
Typhoon, 17, 18, 80, 198, 199, 216, 217

UGUISU, "nightingale of Japan," 128
Ujina, port of Hiroshima, 183, 186, 196, 213
"Union Church," Kobe, 141–143
University, at Tôkyô, 100–102
Uno, province of, 140
Utsunomiya, 188
Uyeno, park, 82–87; station, 116

VANCOUVER, 2, 6, 10–13, 15; inlet of, 19; rivalry with Victoria, 20; 230
Vaulx, Count Henry de la, 229
"Venice of Japan," 144
Venus, a Japanese, 99
Victoria, B.C., 19, 20, 226
Volcanic rocks, 160
Volcano, the next, 61

WAITING-MAIDS, 67, 68, 111, 208
Wakamiya, temple of, 164
War, return of the troops from the, 43, 62, 77, 138, 139, 182, 186; Japanese conduct of the, 195
Warren, Archdeacon, 165
———, Rev. C. F., 166, 167
"Water-cure" for sin, 110
Wayo-tei, Matsuyama, 202–209
Webb, Rev. A. E., 93
Welsh place-names, 8
Western Mail, 1
'Westward to the Far East,' Miss Scidmore's, 17, 205, 206
Will Adams, 44, 45, 186, 187
Wing, Mr. Yung, 4, 5
Winnipeg, 5–7

Wycklife Mission, Canadian, 222

XAVIER, ST. FRANCIS, 245, 246

YAAMI'S, Kyôto, 153
Yama, Regent of the Dead, 169
Yamashina, Prince, at Kyôto Exhibition, 148
Yankee characteristics, 4
Yedo, 49, 79; story of, 80
Yellow Sea, course of typhoon, 17
Yen; see "Currency."
Yodogawa, River, 148
Yokohama, arrival at, 29; native quarter, 33; settlement, 34; foreign population and clubs, 35; churches, 36; distance from Tôkyô, 40; from Kobe, 137; return to, 224; embarkation, 225
Yoritomo, Shôgun, 47
Yoshiwara, the, 113–115
Yumoto (Hakone), 64, 65, 75, 76; (Nikkô), 127–134
Yunomine, 57

ZOOLOGICAL GARDENS, Tôkyô, 86

LONDON: PRINTED BY WILLIAM CLOWES AND SONS, LIMITED,
STAMFORD STREET AND CHARING CROSS.

www.ingramcontent.com/pod-product-compliance
Lightning Source LLC
Chambersburg PA
CBHW031939230426
43672CB00010B/1981